MW01264818

one thing
I DESIRE

"What doth the LORD require of thee,

but to do justly, and to love mercy,

& to *walk humbly* with thy God?"

micah 6 : 8

"All have sinned,

& come *short* of the glory of God."

romans 3 : 23

"Herein is *love*,

not that we loved God, but that He loved us,

& sent his Son to be the

propitiation for our sins."

1 john 4:10

"I am the Lord thy God

Which brought thee out of the land of Egypt:

open thy mouth *wide*, and I will *fill* it."

psalm 81:10

one thing
I DESIRE

to KNOW *C*HRIST *more*

by SARAH L. BRYANT

KR
MINISTRIES

One Thing I Desire
⌒ To Know Christ More

KBR MINISTRIES is a ministry designed to encourage young ladies to grow in accordance with Titus Two and Proverbs 31:10-31, in obedience to God and their parents. For more information, contact:

20767 Z Road | Holton, Kansas 66436
Editor@KingsBloomingRose.com
www.KingsBloomingRose.com

PRINTED in the United States of America

FIRST PRINTING · 2012

ISBN · 978-1-4675-3915-9

SCRIPTURE QUOTATIONS · King James Version of *The Holy Bible*

DEFINITIONS · *American Dictionary of the English Language* by Noah Webster

PHOTOGRAPHY & BOOK DESIGN · ©Sarah Lee Bryant Photo & Design

CALLIGRAPHY · Sarah Hulslander

ALSO BY THIS AUTHOR ·
The Family Daughter: Becoming Pillars of Strength in Our Father's House

dedicated to....

CHRIST JESUS MY LORD

Creator who sustains every breath

Redeemer who paid our ransom

King exalted at the Father's right hand

"Worthy is the Lamb that was slain to receive

power, and riches, and wisdom, and strength,

and honour, and glory, & blessing."

revelation 5:12

"one thing

have I desired LORD, that will I seek after;

that I may dwell in the house

of the LORD all the days of my life,

to *behold the beauty*

of the LORD."

~

psalm 27:4

thank you to....

MY HEAVENLY FATHER & SAVIOR

You sustain my every breath and have given me eternal life—
may You receive all glory and praise forever

MY WONDERFUL PARENTS

thank you for your love and example of obedience to the Lord;
I thank Him for giving me such godly parents

BIBLICAL TEACHERS

Dr. Baucham, Mr. Leiter, Dr. Talbot, Mr. Washer—
thank you for proclaiming the Word of Truth

&

GODLY MENTORS

Mrs. Buckingham, Mrs. Chancey, Mrs. Larsen, Mrs. Morgan, Mrs. Weinhold—
thank you for speaking God's faithfulness and wisdom into my life

Sola deo Gloria!

"Many, O LORD my God,
are Thy *wonderful works* which Thou hast done."

p s a l m   4 0 : 5

"I count all things but

loss for the excellency of the

knowledge of Christ Jesus my Lord...

that I may know Him

and the power of His resurrection,

and the fellowship of His sufferings,

being made conformable unto His death."

∽

p h i l i p p i a n s   3 : 1 0

dear beloved sisters,

WHAT IS YOUR deepest desire—your one predominant longing? What captivates your heart? The apostle Paul said with confidence, "*I count all things but loss for the excellency of the knowledge of Christ Jesus my Lord,*" for he was willing to lay down *all* things for *One* Thing: "*that I may know Him, and the power of His resurrection, and the fellowship of His sufferings, being made conformable unto His death*" (Philippians 3:8,10). Of all the things this man could have desired, knowing Christ Jesus was his greatest yearning—one for which he was willing to give his life.

Where do *you* stand? Is your heart guided by a preeminent yearning to know your Redeemer more deeply and to love Him more passionately? To love the Lord our God is "*the first and great commandment,*" as Jesus Christ says in Matthew 22:37: "*Thou shalt love the Lord thy God with all thy heart, and with all thy soul, and with all thy mind.*" The love we are to have for the Lord is a burning passion kindled in the very core of our being. It is a "first love"—that white-hot love—which is the strongest and most binding (Deuteronomy 6:5). Oh, that our hearts would hold this unalloyed ardor for the Lord our God!

However, how can we love a God we do not know? How can our life bend in sacrificial worship if we have not first sought His face and caught a glimpse of His enrapturing beauties?

The Scriptures reveal God's nature and infallible character to mankind. The mercy contained in this reality is unspeakable, for in so doing, a magnificent Creator stoops to reveal Himself to His own creatures. One of the most merciful beckonings of all time is found in Isaiah 55:6: *"Seek ye the LORD while He may be found, call ye upon Him while He is near."* The eternal God has offered to show us great things without number, if we would but turn from the frivolous things of this world and seek His face (Jeremiah 9:23-24).

Yet, how many of us earnestly seek to know Him? The Lord has promised to show Himself to those who *"seek Him with the whole heart"* (Psalm 119:2)—but have we hidden ourselves away with Him and poured ourselves out in study of the Scriptures? Are our Bibles stained with tears of overflowing gratefulness and marked with the Holy Spirit's teaching? We hear and talk much of Christianity today—we know how to fit in the right Christian circles, read the right books, and say all of the right things—but do we actually know the true Redeemer? Are we truly enraptured by One Thing—the Gospel of Jesus Christ and His glory?

My earnest prayer is that you would catch sight of the Lord God in His Word, so that His love manifested through the Gospel would kindle a life-gripping adoration and gratitude for the wondrous works He has performed on your account (Psalm 103:2-4). As you commit your life to diligently seeking His face in the Scriptures, true joy will fill your days and follow you throughout eternity. Let us humbly sit at the Well of illuminating truth, and beseech its Author to *"open Thou mine eyes, that I may behold wondrous things out of Thy law"* (Psalm 119:18). Truly, *"He is a rewarder of them that diligently seek Him,"* and is eager to instruct us in His perfect way (Psalm 18:32). The more that our hearts see of God revealed in His Word, the more we will be spurred to love

Him—and to dedicate our every breath to "*know Him, and the power of His resurrection*" (Philippians 3:10).

In this book, I feel like an inarticulate infant trying to sketch what I cannot even fully grasp—how can one wrap his mind around the greatness of One Who extends the boundless heavens? How can a finite human plumb the eternal depths of the Gospel which has been authored by an infinite God? I am as one peering through a small keyhole at the entire universe of the Lord and His truth—however, what I have already seen through the Scriptures has captivated my heart! Because of what Christ has accomplished for me on the cross of Calvary, this life is a quest to know Him more each day, driven by a yearning to love Him more passionately as He commands (Deuteronomy 10:12). My heart thrills to realize that these fleeting hours on earth are just an inviting taste of what will be mine to track down throughout all of eternity—the depths of the abounding love and glory of Jesus Christ my Redeemer.

May you too be a joyful captive of this One Thing, propelled by its grandeur—echoing the psalmist, "*One thing have I desired of the LORD, that will I seek after; that I may dwell in the house of the LORD all the days of my life, to behold the beauty of the LORD*" (Psalm 27:4,8).

In Christ Alone,

Sarah Lee

July 2012

"Teach me Thy way,
O LORD; I will walk in Thy truth:
unite my heart to fear Thy name."

psalm 86:11

"Oh, study not God in the jeweled Heavens...

study Him in the *cross of Jesus!*

Look at Him through this wondrous telescope,

and although, as through a glass darkly,

you behold His *glory*—

the Godhead in awful eclipse,

the sun of His deity setting in blood—

yet that rude and crimsoned cross

more fully *reveals the mind* of God."

o c t a v i u s   w i n s l o w

one

looking *unto Jesus*

We are only given one life—one brief season of time to spend on earth. The average human life span of 78 years is but a blink of an eye in light of a shoreless eternity. James 4:14 soberly reminds us, *"What is your life? It is even a vapour, that appeareth for a little time, and then vanisheth away."* Even the most accomplished, exceptionally-influential men of renown die; their life's timeline begins with their date of birth, chronicles major life occurrences or achievements, and however impressive that repertoire is, undoubtedly concludes with their death date. Likewise, in just a few short days, we too will stand at the sunset of our life's lamp and will realize the momentary length of the one earthly life that we have been given.

With this comprehension, we must ask—how should we then live? What is of lasting value to seek during this fleeting earthly life? Should not our desire be to live profitably, since we are given only one transient moment in which to do so?

As C.T. Studd once penned the answer, "Only one life, 'twill soon be past; only what's done for Christ will last." We are only given one supreme, over-arching, ultimate reason for which to live—God and Christ alone. Why, one might ask, should we give everything we have to Him? The answer is found in Titus 2:11—*"the grace of God that bringeth salvation hath appeared to all men"*! This one truth should cause our hearts to palpitate with inexpressible joy, for though we were once drowning in the pit of self-induced sin, we are not left hopeless in our own filth.

Sin's intoxicating presence separates man from communion with a God Who is unsurpassingly holy and righteous. *"There is none righteous, no, not one"* (Romans 3:10), and because *"the wages of sin is death"* (Romans 6:23), every one of us deserves eternal punishment for our rebellion against a righteous Creator.

Yet—the grace of God has brought salvation to mankind! A Mediator and Redeemer came to rescue us from the smothering pit of our iniquities and to restore our broken relationship with the Lord God. Blood was required for that reconciliation: the very blood of the Lord's own Son, for in the process of freeing man from his deserved eternal punishment, Jesus Christ had to bear it Himself. *"To the Lord our God belong mercies and forgiveness, though we have rebelled against Him"* (Daniel 9:9). What a grand exhibition of infinite love is revealed in this truth—this is the greatest wonder in the universe!

journey of a lifetime

Just who is this Jesus Christ? Who is this God-man Who redeemed us from eternal death? As Psalm 8:4 asks, *"What is man, that Thou art mindful of him? and the son of man, that Thou visitest him?"* Why did the One against Whom we have viciously rebelled reach down to rescue us from the miry pit of sin?

This is the question that has captivated the hearts and lives of God's people throughout the ages. It is the quest of an entire lifetime, which propels the believing heart to seek out its depths.

In His sovereign mercy, our redeeming God authored (II Peter 1:21) an entire volume—the Bible—which unfolds His redemptive plan throughout the course of history. All are beckoned to come and search its truth, *"for the commandment is a lamp; and the law is light"* (Proverbs 6:23). In the Living Word, the curtain is drawn back and the tip of the enormous iceberg of Christ's vast glory is revealed to our wondering eyes. However, to grasp the fullness of the Son's sacrifice required for our salvation, we must first catch a glimpse of His glory, love, and unity with the Father before His incarnation—before the eternal Son of God embodied Himself in human flesh.

everlasting son of God

"In the beginning was the Word, and the Word was with God, and the Word was God. The same was in the beginning with God. All things were made by Him; and without Him was not any thing made that was made" (John 1:1-4). John here tells us that Jesus Christ— "the Word" (Revelation 19:14)—existed from eternity past with God the Father, with whom He has exhaustive unity and combined power. *"I and my Father are one"* (John 10:30). Christ the Son (Matthew 26:64) has dwelt with the Father before time even began, abiding in a perfect bond of ultimate sovereignty, holiness, and undivided communing love. Their uninterrupted union brims with love flowing cohesively to and from one another (John 15:9). God has always perfectly loved His Son with a love that could never be compared to any human affection—an infinite, holy, satisfying love (John 17:23); the Father has always done everything for His Son's glory and pleasure (Colossians 1:19) and the Son has always loved and willingly submitted to His Father (Luke 3:22).

creator of all things

The Godhead's ocean of love and unity overflowed as the birth of *all* created things. This act was a grand demonstration to all mankind of Their united love and mercy (Colossians 1:16)— *"by His Son, whom He hath appointed heir of all things, by whom also He made the worlds"* (Hebrews 1:2). God did not *need* the universe, the complex designs of the stars, or the beauties of a tiny wild rose—but He created entire worlds for His Son's glory and *delight.* Colossians 1:19 says, *"It pleased the Father that in Him should all fulness dwell."* From the depths of the heavens' galaxies, to the minutest compo-

christ in colossians one

Transforms us into His kingdom (1:13)

Redeems us through His blood (1:14)

Reflects image of invisible God (1:15)

Has preeminence over all (15-18)

Receives glory through creation (1:16)

Sustains the world (1:17)

Preeminent head of church body (1:18)

Reconciles all things to Himself through His blood (1:20)

Presents us as holy in His sight (1:22)

Reveals the mystery once hidden (1:27)

Gives us hope of glory (1:27)

Works mightily (1:29)

nent in a leaf, Christ is the purpose and origin of its intricate design. The power of this verity and demonstration of God's love humbles the heart of the believer!

sustainer of life

The Lord God did not create this world and leave it to continue without His guidance and power; Colossians 1:17 says that by Jesus Christ *"all things consist."* This reveals that the immeasurable power of Christ is spilled forth constantly in the creation of the world, for His entity is its moment-by-moment sustaining force. If we sew a quilt, our presence is not required for it to maintain the same form after its completion. This is because we use materials that consist and maintain their form without our support. However, because the Lord created every atom from *nothing*—something we could never do—He is the only power which sustains and orders its course. Herein is revealed the absolute sovereignty and power of Jesus Christ, and what a glorious truth this is to grasp. Commenting on Colossians 1:17, John Gill wrote, "Yea, all mankind live and move, and have their being in [Christ]." Hebrews 1:3 says Christ is *"upholding all things by the word of His power."* His continuing power in creation is enforced throughout each millisecond simply by His word! Without His hand, all things would simply vanish into vapor. As William S. Plumer wrote, "All creatures....hang dependent on His powerful providence and if one link in the chain of that dependence were broken, they would all rush headlong to destruction!"

"For by Him were all things created, that are in heaven, and that are in earth, visible and invisible, whether they be thrones, or dominions, or principalities, or powers: all things were created by Him, and for Him" (Colossians 1:16). From His heavenly throne, Christ guides the orbit path of universes, galaxies, and planets—as well as unknown worlds, invisible thrones, dominions, principalities, powers, angels, and kingdoms (John 17:2). This He does without effort or strain! It overwhelms one's mind to think of the strength contained in the command of these activities, and that the exertion does not drain His capabilities in the smallest way (John 19:11, Colossians 2:10). Can you imagine the burdens that continually weigh upon a country's president? His decisions determine the course of countless variables and lives; however, in all of his responsibilities and power, many committees assist him

and put his commands into action. In a much greater way, Jesus Christ supremely reigns over all created things, over every kingdom, culture, church, and life—down to the smallest plant and animal—without effort nor assistance. I Corinthians 8:6 says, *"To us there is but one God, the Father, of whom are all things, and we in Him; and one Lord Jesus Christ, by whom are all things, and we by Him."* Our every breath is granted by the power of the Lord. How true is Psalm 145:15 when it speaks of creation's reliance on its Creator: *"The eyes of all wait upon Thee; and Thou givest them their meat in due season."* The more I see of the Lord's power revealed throughout His creation, the more I bow in the reality of my unworthiness to even utter His name! *"O come, let us worship and bow down: let us kneel before the LORD our maker"* (Psalm 95:6).

culprits of the curse

After the creation of the universe, *"God saw every thing that He had made, and, behold, it was very good"* (Genesis 1:31). The Lord had established by His own hand a beautiful, unmarred world of revolving order, and everything contained in it glorified its Maker by fulfilling its divinely-appointed purpose.

Everything—that is, except mankind, the crowning work of His creation. *"God said, Let us make man in our image, after our likeness: and let them have dominion over the fish of the sea, and over the fowl of the air, and over the cattle, and over all the earth, and over every creeping thing that creepeth upon the earth"* (Genesis 1:26). *"God created man in His own image"* (Genesis 1:27), thus man was the only creature made in God's likeness, given a soul and a mind to adore his Creator. As a moral agent, man possessed the ability to understand and reason, unlike animals. Man's ultimate purpose was to glorify his Maker and take dominion over creation (I Corinthians 6:20). However, as we know from Genesis chapter three, Adam and Eve brought sin[1]—the corruption and defilement of disobedience—into God's perfect world through flagrant, willing rebellion against His command not to partake of the tree of life. The Lord had provided all that they needed in the garden of Eden; nonetheless, *"when the woman saw that the tree was good for food, and that it was pleasant to the eyes, and a tree to be desired to make one wise, she took of the fruit thereof, and did eat, and gave also unto her husband with her; and he did eat,"* says Genesis 3:6. As our *"first father hath sinned"* (Isaiah 43:27), disobediently reaching out to eat of this forbidden fruit, he invited upon himself and upon the entire human race the perfectly just punishment of God, for he had chosen to violate from his Creator's will. *"Wherefore, as by one man sin entered into the world, and death by sin; and so death passed upon all men, for that all have sinned"* (Romans 5:12).

Since this fall into sin, every son of Adam has been born with this sin nature and has rebelled against his Creator throughout every self-lived moment (Psalm 58:3). Mankind has done nothing but rebel against the perfect order which God established in His creation (Jeremiah 17:9, Romans 3:12). As Proverbs 20:9 asks, *"Who can say, I have made my heart clean, I am pure from my sin?"* Man's desire has been to become free of God's authority, accountability, and power—although it is the very force that sustains his every breath. *"The God in whose hand thy breath is, and whose are all thy ways, hast thou not glorified"* (Daniel 5:23). We have not just committed one sin against the Lord, but we have broken *every* commandment of God (Matthew 5:19-48) given in Exodus chapter twenty, either in thought or deed—the greatest being to *"love the LORD thy God with all thine heart, and*

---

[1] SIN. *Voluntary departure of a moral agent from a known rule of rectitude or duty, prescribed by God.*

with all thy soul, and with all thy might" (Deuteronomy 6:5). Not one man, except the Lord Jesus Christ, has ever loved God in perfect obedience to this command. We were made to glorify God and to live for Him alone (I Corinthians 6:19), and yet in our sin, we walk in conclusive contradiction to that intent. *"There is none righteous, no, not one"* (Romans 3:10). We may not want to admit the desperately wretched state of our souls which are covered with sin, but the truth is that our iniquities weigh us down into a horrible pit, from which we cannot escape on our own power (Psalm 40:2). *"For mine iniquities are gone over mine head: as an heavy burden they are too heavy for me"* (Psalm 38:4). How can a God that is holy (Leviticus 11:44), righteous (Psalm 11:7), and just (Psalm 89:14) behold the monstrous presence of sin in His once-perfect created order?

what does a good God...

We see a picture of the Lord's impeccable holiness—separation from sin—from the proclamation of the seraphim in Isaiah chapter six: *"I saw also the Lord sitting upon a throne, high and lifted up, and His train filled the temple. Above it stood the seraphims: each one had six wings; with twain he covered his face, and with twain he covered his feet, and with twain he did fly. And one cried unto another, and said, Holy, holy, holy, is the LORD of hosts."* The seraphim, who are sinless, have such a realization of their own "createdness," that they cover their faces and feet, in a desire to point to and worship the One with non-created holiness. From their proclamation of "Holy, holy, holy," we catch a peek of the worthy purity of God Almighty, Whose impeccability is radiated in every turn. The holiness of the Lord is not simply a lack of sin's presence in His nature, but it is the completely separated, sanctified, and hallowed purity of His Being. His holiness is far beyond our finite comprehension, as Winslow wrote, "Only as we keep our eye upon atoning blood, can we for a moment gaze upon the unsufferable brightness of the God of holiness."

Thus, how could a wholly good God be neutral about sin? How can one Who hates wickedness and loves righteousness overlook the rebellion of culprits who have dishonored Him throughout every breath and are infiltrated with their own filth (Ephesians 5:5)?

> The very fact that this world has green grass and sustaining water is a witness of Christ's engulfing *love & mercy.*

...do with sinners?

A gloriously holy God cannot overlook man's sin; Psalm 7:11 says that "*God is angry with the wicked every day,*" for He "*hast loved righteousness, and hated iniquity*" (Hebrews 1:9). Proverbs 15:9 says that "*the way of the wicked is an abomination unto the LORD*" (Proverbs 15:9); the word "abomination" in the Scriptures conveys the fiercest level of God's abhorrence and detestation. Therefore, in justice, God must pour forth the rightful punishment due to man's iniquities; this cataclysm is described in Psalm 75:8: "*In the hand of the LORD there is a cup, and the wine is red; it is full of mixture; and He poureth out of the same: but the dregs thereof, all the wicked of the earth shall wring them out, and drink them.*" This is the full cup of God's wrath—perfectly merited and wholly just—which must be poured out upon every sinner in recompense for his transgressions against a good and righteous Creator (Jeremiah 7:20). As Charles Leiter says, "God's wrath is not a temporary loss of self-control or a selfish fit of emotion. It is His holy, white-hot hatred of sin." "*The wages of sin is death*"—if that were the end of the story, we all would be hopelessly, but justly, condemned (Nahum 1:2)—yet! that verse is not the end of God's message, for Romans 6:23 continues, *"but the gift of God is eternal life through Jesus Christ our Lord."*

what manner of love

Against all hope, we see a radiant spark of deliverance offered by none other than the One we transgressed against: God Himself! Though He is a God of perfect justice and holiness, His mercy and love are also infinite; in His overflowing grace, the Lord purposed to reconcile mankind through a glorious plan of redemption. Therefore, the Lord initiated a legal propitiation[2]—a payment for the His justice toward man's sin—so that His people would stand before Himself in favor. *"Whom God hath set forth to be a propitiation through faith in His blood, to declare His righteousness for the remission of sins that are past, through the forbearance of God"* (Romans 3:25).

> The moving cause of the *incarnation* of Christ is the love of the Father and of the Son to mankind.
>
> (JOHN GILL)

There was found no man without sin who could redeem the course of mankind as a perfect propitiation, nor was there a man who could drink down the cup of God's infinite wrath. No one, except the Lord Himself! God's own beloved Son—united with Him in uncontained power, infinite glory, and impeccable holiness (John 10:30)—broke into time two thousand years ago, and clothed Himself with human flesh in submission to His Father. *"God commendeth His love toward us, in that, while we were yet sinners, Christ died for us"* (Romans 5:8).

Entering into a realm He had never before been, Jesus

---

[2] PROPITIATION. *The atonement or atoning sacrifice offered to God to assuage His wrath and render Him propitious to sinners.*

Christ limited Himself to humanity to serve (Matthew 25:40) and ultimately bear the punishment of the very ones who rebelled against Him (Isaiah 53:3). This demonstration of love leaves one prostrate in worship, for the very act of entering this cursed world was a deep humiliation for the Son of the eternal God. Psalm 113:6 says it is a condescension for the Lord to even look at earth: *"Who humbleth Himself to behold the things that are in heaven, and in the earth!"* In this mission, the Son submitted willingly to the Father's plan of redemption (Matthew 26:42).

Why would God, the precious reason and means of our existence, undertake this mission? The Lord sent forth His beloved Son as a grand demonstration of His rich mercy and mighty grace to those who deserved nothing but punishment. *"God, who is rich in mercy, for His great love wherewith He loved us, even when we were dead in sins, hath quickened us together with Christ...That in the ages to come He might shew the exceeding riches of His grace in His kindness toward us through Christ Jesus"* (Ephesians 2:4-5,7). The Lord Almighty desired to cleanse and transform the hopeless into a holy people for Himself, to bring glory to His name through the unmerited sacrifice of His Son. Deuteronomy 14:2 says, *"The LORD hath chosen thee to be a peculiar people unto Himself."* The sacrifice involved in establishing a salvation plan is a vivid and undeniable showcase of God's incredible love for His people. As He chose to lavish His gift of salvation, love, and grace upon the wretched and undeserving, all who realize this wonder will turn in praise of His overwhelming goodness (Psalm 103:2-3). Jeremiah 33:9 says that God's people *"shall be to Me a name of joy, a praise and an honour before all the nations of the earth, which shall hear all the good that I do unto them."*

As the promised Messiah, Jesus Christ's life on earth was one of perfect submission to God. His ultimate goal was to *"be* about [His] Father's business" (Luke 2:49). Wholly loving and obeying His God, Jesus led a spotless life, one worthy of no condemnation (Revelation 15:3). The Son of God was the only sinless, perfect man Who ever walked the face of this earth.

However, on one dark night, God did something He had never before done in eternity past: He turned His face away from His perfect Son. The Father legally imputed[3] to Christ the condemning sin of the entire world; I John 2:2 says, *"[Christ] is the propitiation for our sins: and not for ours only, but also for the sins of the whole world."* As He was taken to the hill of Calvary and crucified on a tree, Jesus was forsaken to bear the curse of God's law, not for any transgression He had committed, but for man's iniquities. The only One worthy to be blessed bore the Mosaic curse we deserve, found in Deuteronomy 18:16-20:

> *Notice the references of suffering in Isaiah 53. The pain of the Cross causes one to bow in worship— Christ's great sacrifice for our salvation!*

> *"Cursed shalt thou be in the city, and cursed shalt thou be in the field. Cursed shall be thy basket and thy store. Cursed shall be the fruit of thy body, and the fruit of thy land, the increase of thy kine, and the flocks of thy sheep. Cursed shalt thou be when thou comest in, and cursed shalt thou be when thou goest out. The LORD shall send upon thee cursing, vexation, and rebuke...until thou perish quickly."*

Despite the pain of the Cross, the Son submitted to God's will, *"Father, if Thou be willing, remove this cup from Me: nevertheless not My will, but Thine, be done"* (Luke 22:42). Jesus Christ was cut

---

[3] IMPUTED. *To charge; to attribute; to reckon what does not belong to him.*

off from the Father; He was stricken, smitten, and afflicted; He was wounded, bruised and chastised; He was beaten, oppressed, afflicted—He poured out His soul unto death as an offering for man's transgressions (Isaiah 53).

While all of Heaven watched in astonishment, the King took the penalty of the traitor; the Highest took the place of the lowest; as the Prince of Glory gave His life for the wicked. As He was crucified on Calvary (Luke 23:33), Jesus cried out, *"Eli, Eli, lama*

> He drank a cup of wrath without *mercy* so we might drink a cup of mercy without *wrath.*

sabachthani? that is to say, My God, My God, why hast Thou forsaken Me?" (Matthew 27:46) Although later the apostle Paul would victoriously claim, *"We are troubled on every side, yet not distressed; we are perplexed, but not in despair; persecuted, but not forsaken; cast down, but not destroyed"* (II Corinthians 4:8-9), Christ's lot was to be troubled, distressed, cursed, forsaken, and destroyed there on the tree (Mark 15:30). This was the estrangement from the Lord God that we, for our sin, should bear; *"yet it pleased the LORD to bruise [Christ]; He hath put Him to grief: when Thou shalt make His soul an offering for sin"* (Isaiah 53:10). The Lord unleashed this pain upon His beloved Son's back, as He bore our vile iniquities (II Corinthians 5:21). The piercing magnitude of Jesus' sacrifice—to be rejected by the Father Who had throughout all of eternity loved Him—is far beyond anything we can ever fathom.

Yet, we see no deficiency in our Savior. He drank down that immense cup of God's righteous wrath to the very dregs without flinching. He cried out at last, *"It is finished"* (John 19:30)—it was complete! Jesus had conquered death through His shed blood, and established the only way of man's redemption. *"Sacrifice and offering and burnt offerings and offering for sin* thou wouldest not, neither hadst pleasure therein...we are sanctified through the offering of the body of Jesus Christ once for all" (Hebrews 10:8,10). Oh, love "so amazing and so divine"!

Three days after His death on the cross, Christ Jesus victoriously arose from the grave, for death held no power over the Maker of all things. Matthew 28:5-6 records the angel's words to the women who beheld His empty tomb: *"Fear not ye: for I know that ye seek Jesus, which was crucified. He is not here: for He is risen, as He said."* Christ was wholly victorious over sin, and is now *"set down at the right hand of the throne of God"* (Hebrews 12:2), highly exalted *"far above all principality, and power, and might, and dominion, and every name that is named"* (Ephesians 1:21). *"Worthy is the Lamb that was slain to receive power, and riches, and wisdom, and strength, and honour, and glory, and blessing"* (Revelation 5:12)!

only thread of hope

As the holy Judge and the worthy Lamb, Christ has promised to someday return to this world, to judge the living and the dead (Ezekiel 18:30). We are warned that the *"day of the Lord will come as a thief in the night; in the which the heavens shall pass away with a great noise"* (II Peter 3:10).

> Are you known of *God?*
> (GALATIANS 4:9)

Jesus Christ—the Way, the Truth, and the Life (John 14:6)—now commands all men to repent from their sins and believe in His finished work for their salvation, beckoning, *"Whosoever shall call upon the name of the Lord shall be saved"* (Romans 10:13). Realizing your own rebellion against your Creator, have you turned from your sin unto His righteousness? II Corinthians 7:10 says, *"For godly sorrow worketh repentance to salvation not to be repented of."* Have you ever truly put your soul's trust for eternal salvation in Christ for the ransom of your vast sins? He is your only source of hope. If you are standing outside of Jesus' all-sufficient sacrifice, on judgment day (Revelation 6:17), you will be forced to drink the just punishment of your rebellion against your Maker, for *"the wages of sin is death"* (Romans 6:23). In His consuming presence, every "good deed" will melt, leaving spiritually naked

> Christ's blood is offered for the atonement— the *covering*—of our sins.

any who bear not the clothing of Christ's mercy (II Corinthians 5:3). In all of our "good works," in all of our put-on manners and culture, we are *nothing* outside of Christ, for *"no man is justified by the law in the sight of God"* (Galatians 3:11). Ezekiel 18:30 pleads, *"Repent, and turn yourselves from all your transgressions; so iniquity shall not be your ruin."*

Isaiah 64:6 likens us *"all as an unclean thing, and all our righteousnesses are as filthy rags."* In our sin, we are like nauseating, repulsive *revolting* rags to the Lord of holiness! Man's "righteousness" is false bluff before a holy, all-consuming God of fire (Hebrews 12:29). He knows every thought that has ever or will enter our head (Psalm 139:1). How deep would your embarrassment be if your every thought was exposed to your friends? If you would feel shame to be exposed to other sinful beings, how will you stand in the presence of a *holy* and omniscient[4] God Who knows you inside and out? *"If thou sayest, Behold, we knew it not; doth not He that pondereth the heart consider it? and He that keepeth thy soul, doth not He know it? and shall not He render to every*

---

[4] OMNISCIENT. *Having universal knowledge; infinitely knowing.*

man according to his works?" (Proverbs 24:12)

In modern western evangelical Christianity, the truths of man's depravity and God's absolute righteous justice are often omitted in the "Gospel" presentation—but how can one realize the greatness of Christ's atoning gift in salvation unless seen through the hopelessness of man's corrupt condition? Who can begin to know the immeasurable gift contained in God's promise that *"whosoever shall call upon the name of the Lord shall be saved"* (Romans 10:13), without first a realization of our incurable dark state outside of His mercy?

Your only hope from eternal destruction is to trust in Jesus Christ, the victorious Godman (Hebrews 4:15) Who bore your curse. In John 14:6 He says, *"I am the way, the truth, and the life: no man cometh unto the Father, but by Me."* You must trust and believe in the Son of God as your only eternal hope, knowing that apart from His emancipating blood, you will be found guilty before the righteous Judge (Psalm 96:13, Revelation 20:15). If you have never truly placed your trust in Him and surrendered your life to Jesus as your Savior, do so now. As your Creator, Sustainer and Redeemer, God has a claim upon you (Isaiah 45:9). Isaiah 43:7 says, *"Even every one that is called by My name: for I have created him for My glory, I have formed him; yea, I have made him,"* therefore, you are not living on this earth for your own gratification, but rather for the glory of your Maker. (I Corinthians 6:19) Your breath at this moment is sustained by Christ alone (Isaiah 45:9). *"What? know ye not that your body is the temple of the Holy Ghost which is in you, which ye*

> He is *Lord* of lords, and *King* of kings: and they that are with Him are called, and chosen, and faithful.
>
> (REVELATION 17:14)

have of God, and ye are not your own?" Turn to Him for salvation; though God knows your every sin, He still loves you and desires that none should perish without His Son. *"Even so it is not the will of your Father which is in Heaven, that one of these little ones should perish"* (Matthew 18:14). Cry out to the Lord, *"I will declare mine iniquity; I will be sorry for my sin"* (Psalms 38:18).Turn away from your sins and embrace Christ's sovereign lordship over your life. *"If thou shalt confess with thy mouth the Lord Jesus, and shalt believe in thine heart that God hath raised Him from the dead, thou shalt be saved"* (Romans 10:9).

II Corinthians 5:17 says, *"If any man be in Christ, he is a new creature: old things are passed away; behold, all things are become new."* When you become a new creature in Jesus Christ, your former heart of stone is replaced with *"an heart of flesh"* (Ezekiel 11:19), and will continue to be sanctified in the righteousness through the work of the Holy Spirit.

captain of our salvation

When we are known of God and clothed in Christ's righteousness, we are justified before His throne and promised eternal life with Him. *"Being justified freely by His grace through the redemption that is in Christ Jesus"* (Romans 3:24). Because our sins were imputed to Christ's account on that tree two thousand years ago, when He bore our deserved punishment, His righteousness is now laid upon us, as His people. *"Therefore being justified by faith, we have peace with God through our Lord Jesus Christ"* (Romans 5:1). Through the overflowing storehouses of Christ's priceless riches (Ephesians 3:8), the complete ransom price of everyone ever to come to His name (Philippians 4:19) is "paid in full." *"Though He was rich, yet for your sakes He became poor, that ye through His poverty might be rich"* (II Corinthians 8:9). There is no judgment left for Christ's people—no after-reckonings. *"There is therefore now no condemnation to them which are in Christ Jesus, who walk not after the flesh, but after the Spirit"* (Romans 8:1). Psalm 103:12 glories in this truth, *"As far as the east is from the west, so far hath He removed our transgressions from us."* From the heinous sins of Abraham, David, Paul, and all of God's people throughout history down to you and I, a holy God can now forgive their transgressions—because He gave His own Son as a sacrifice. *"I, even I, am He that blotteth out thy transgressions for Mine own sake, and will not remember thy sins"* (Isaiah 43:25). The enormity of Christ's payment demonstrates how much God hates sin, as well as the depths of His mercy in our justification. *"Beloved, now are we the sons of God, and...when He shall appear, we shall be like Him; for we shall see Him as He is"* (I John 3:2). We can now anticipate the day we meet our Maker in Heaven—not for judgment, but for a joyful welcome—and shall worship Him face to face (Psalm 116:15).

For this immense joy, we can *"greatly rejoice in the LORD, my soul shall be joyful in my God; for He hath clothed me with the garments of salvation, He hath covered me with the robe of righteousness"* (Isaiah 61:10). Revel in the beauty of Isaiah 43:1-2: *"Fear not: for I have redeemed thee, I have called thee by thy name; thou art Mine. When thou passest through the waters, I will be with thee; and through the rivers, they shall not overflow thee: when thou walkest through the fire, thou shalt not be burned; neither shall the flame kindle upon thee."* The One Who has saved us will never forsake us, especially in the hardest trials of life. How I love Psalm 63:7—*"Because Thou hast been my help, therefore in the shadow of Thy wings will I rejoice"*! What a joy and comfort it is to live in the shelter of our great High Priest Who ransomed us, not for anything we have done, but because of His ounchanging love. Never can we be condemned or taken from His grip of love. Romans 8:39 majestically says that *"Neither death, nor life, nor angels, nor principalities, nor powers, nor things present, nor things to come, nor height, nor depth, nor any other creature, shall be able to separate us from the love of God, which is in Christ Jesus our Lord."* There is tremendous security in being found in Christ, Who will forever keep us under His wing and bring us to dwell in His holy Palace one day (John 14:2).

After we are saved by Christ, to doubt our salvation is to question the sufficiency of His sacrifice. Do not allow the "accuser of the brethren" (Revelation 12:10) take your eyes from Jesus, for his accusations are vain. Yes, we still sin, yes we daily fail; but in our weakness, we run closer to Christ Who promises in II Corinthians 12:9, *"My grace is sufficient for thee: for my strength is made perfect in weakness."* Oh, what a glorious truth! *"In all these things we are more than conquerors through Him that loved us"* (Romans 8:37). We must always look to Him for strength to overcome the battles of life. Let us say with the apostle, *"This one thing I do, forgetting those things which are behind, and reaching forth unto those things which are before, I press toward the mark for the prize of the high calling of God in Christ Jesus"* (Philippians 3:13). Our feelings come and go, but *"Jesus Christ [is] the same yesterday, and to day, and for ever"* (Hebrews 13:8). God loves us with *"an everlasting love"* (Jeremiah 31:3); instead of looking at ourselves and our failures morbidly, we should look to our Potentate[5] (I Timothy 6:15) Who lives and reigns. Our salvation is not about us: it is about our Redeemer! *"Not unto us, O LORD, not unto us, but unto Thy name give glory, for thy mercy, and for Thy truth's sake"* (Psalms 115:1). May we praise God continually *"for His unspeakable gift"* (II Corinthians 9:15)—for we certainly are not worthy of it (Ephesians 2:8).

---

[5] POTENTATE. *A Prince; a sovereign.*

cloud of witnesses

In Isaiah 42:6 God promises, *"I the LORD have called thee in righteousness, and will hold thine hand, and will keep thee."* This testimony has been proven by the saints throughout history. Jacob was a chosen son of God and endured many hardships, yet on the eve of his death, he told his sons about *"the God which fed me all my life long unto this day"* (Genesis 48:15). His testimony shows the faithfulness of God to the Abrahamic covenant. The staunch leader of Israel, Joshua, led God's people for many years as their spokesman, elder, judge, intercessor, and spiritual guide.

He had trusted in One source of provision throughout trials and triumphs, and at the setting of his life's sunset, he proclaimed this powerful testimony of his God: *"Ye know in all your hearts and in all your souls, that not one thing hath failed of all the good things which the LORD your God spake concerning you; all are come to pass unto you,*

> You have to be *captured* by two days: the day when Christ hung before men, & the day when all men will *kneel* before Christ.
> (PAUL WASHER)

and not one thing hath failed thereof" (Joshua 23:14). This man had proven that not *one* of the Lord's words ever failed! David, who had his fair share of suffering, persecution, transgression, and close encounters with death, was unwavering in his trust in the Almighty. He testified in Psalm 37:25, *"I have been young, and now am old; yet have I not seen the righteous forsaken, nor his seed begging bread"*—and at the end of his life, he therefore advised his son, *"Know thou the God of thy father, and serve Him with a perfect heart and with a willing mind"* (I Chronicles 28:9). Solomon himself would later proclaim, *"Blessed be the LORD...there hath not failed one word of all His good promise"* (I Kings 8:56).

The cloud of witnesses that has gone before us have found our Guide to be wholly true and faithful. Hebrews 12:1 spurs us to run the race faithfully until the end: *"Seeing we also are compassed about with so great a cloud of witnesses, let us lay aside every weight, and the sin which doth so easily beset us, and let us run with patience the race that is set before us."* With our eyes ever looking to our Master, may we joyfully lay aside every weight and press forward, guided by His sure hand and inspired by His example: *"Looking unto Jesus the author and finisher of our faith; who for the joy that was set before Him endured the cross, despising the shame, and is set down at the right hand of the throne of God"* (Hebrews 12:2).

a glorious captor

The all-glorious truth of the Gospel—and love of Jesus Christ contained in it—propels the believer to eagerly seek out its depths with awe and joy. May the heavenly calling to plumb the sublime *"blessing of the gospel of Christ"* (Romans 15:29) be our life's solo goal. While our King tarries (John 21:22), let us live to know, love, and serve Him—for He is eternally worthy. *"One thing have I desired...that I may dwell in the house of the LORD all the days of my life, to behold the beauty of the LORD"* (Psalm 27:4).

"As an exhibition of unparalleled *love*,
the Cross melts and captivates the *heart*."

john angell james

"No better employment can

engage heart and hands than,

in the spirit...of prayer and meditation,

of separation from the world, of holy fear,

of a *desire to know* the will of God and do it,

of humility, simplicity, and godly sincerity,

to seek to enter into those heavenly mysteries which

are stored up in the *Scriptures*."

j . c . p h i l p o t

a *captivating quest*

"O the depth of the riches both of the wisdom and knowledge of God! how unsearchable are His judgments, and His ways past finding out!" exclaims Romans 11:33. Truly, the depth of God's wisdom contained in the Gospel is more than our finite minds can ever comprehend; one could spend a hundred lifetimes seeking it out, and only reach the base of its mountainous truth. It is not simply a story which we grasp at the beginning of our walk with Christ, and then continue on to learn "greater" things; rather, it is the *one* thing that we will be seeking to know more fully daily for the rest of our lives. We have been given a tremendous blessing to be able to glimpse its glories unfolded in the infallible Word of God. The more we see of its truths, the more we will find there is yet to grasp; this realization will cause our anticipation to build for that day when Christ Himself will unveil to us the grandeurs of His work accomplished on the Cross.

Our heavenly Father has promised throughout the Scriptures that, "*If from thence thou shalt seek the LORD thy God, thou shalt find Him, if thou seek Him with all thy heart and with all thy soul*" (Deuteronomy 4:29). How awing it is that the Lord of the universe makes Himself to be known by His helpless creatures, and joys to have us seek Him. Jeremiah 29:13 says, *"Ye shall seek Me, and find Me, when ye shall search for Me with all your heart."* God has given us the ability to see His redemptive work through His inspired Word, and as He enlightens our eyes to its wisdom, its power will lead us in the way of righteousness and eternal life. In Romans 1:16 Paul said, *"I am not ashamed of the gospel of Christ: for it is the power of God unto salvation to every one that believeth."* It should be our greatest joy to seek out the Gospel, unveiled in God's Word to us.

that i may know him

Many of us may know *about* God: we read books about Him, we study preachers' and theologians' writings, we read about godly Christians, and we may even know and debate doctrine—but have we really sought to know *Christ* personally through *His* Writing? Where is the reality in our life that we know Him personally? Do we really walk day by day with the One Who has redeemed us, and do we delight in knowing His wondrous attributes?

> *how many* months have you spent studying the attributes of God?

Jeremiah 9:23-24 says that we have nothing to glory in, save in our knowledge of the Lord Almighty. Nothing else truly matters, compared to the Creator of the universe! Listen to these words: *"Let not the wise man glory in his wisdom, neither let the mighty man glory in his might, let not the rich man glory in his riches: but let him that glorieth glory in this, that he understandeth and knoweth me, that I am the LORD which exercise lovingkindness, judgment, and righteousness, in the earth."* The very purpose of our life must be to better know our Lord Jesus and His glorious character. In our minds, we may know that this is essential to our life—yet how much is this truth exhibited in our life? How many hours of the night have you spent on your knees, seeking His face (Psalm 27:4)? Are your life's guiding principles based on your own personal conviction of Biblical truth (II Timothy 1:12)? There is so much God is willing to teach and bestow upon us about Himself and His will, if we will but humble ourselves before Him and ask that He in-struct us (Luke 11:9). As we dig into the well of Scripture's revela-tion of the Gospel, our hearts will become kindled by its glory.

> My soul *thirsteth* for God, for the living God.
> (PSALM 42:1-2)

Christ abundantly *"satisfieth the longing soul, and filleth the hungry soul with goodness"* (Psalm 107:9). For this spiritual filling, the Lord commands us simply to *"open thy mouth wide, and I will fill it"* (Psalm 81:10). He will willingly bestow His illumination when we ask, *"Open thou mine eyes, that I may behold wondrous things out of Thy law. Make me to understand the way of Thy precepts"* (Psalm 119:18, 27). How vividly I remem-ber that spring morning when I pondered these petitions for Scriptural understanding, and begged for the enlightenment of my spiritually-dimmed eyes—a result of my fallen state before God (Romans 3:23)—so that I could understand the truths of His life-giving Word. My heavenly Father has generously granted this plea as I seek His truth day after day; what transforming power is contained in His wisdom. James 1:17 says that *"every good gift and every perfect gift is from above, and cometh down from the Father of lights"*; therefore, we must fall on our knees, humbly asking our King to teach our hungry hearts as we open His Law.

Petition your Savior to fill your parched soul with the hidden treasures of the Gospel (Colossians 1:27), that your heart would be transformed and gripped by its truths.

Christ is revealed through every portion of the Scriptures (II Corinthians 4:4); therefore, as we study, we see clearer glimpses of His illimitable[1] image. I love seeing my Jehovah-Raah[2] unveiled in His Word, where His "fingerprint" is etched in every line. Recording His innumerable traits from the Scriptures has been strengthening to my faith; it is like a sketch being filled in with greater detail, each attribute adding context and contour to His image's enormity. Yet, however awing these revelations of God are, they show only a microscopic portion of His true being. Regardless of how many times we will have read through the Bible and studied God therein in our lifetime, we will have seen only a *fraction* of Himself. This fact powerfully motivates me to seek His face and to faithfully press toward the day when His glory (Matthew 25:31) will be unveiled; Christ prayed in John 17:24, *"Father, I will that they also, whom Thou hast given Me, be with Me where I am; that they may behold My glory."* Like the little girl craning her neck from her window to catch a glimpse of her father's face as he returns from a long journey, may we always, in our study of the Word, be scrambling for another view of our heavenly Redeemer and Lover.

It is a great privilege to be able to know the one true God—the Creator Who created us with His own breath (Genesis 2:7)—in a personal friendship! How would you feel if, after you met a senator or well-known pastor, you were taken into his confidence? Wouldn't you feel honored if he remembered you and sought your assistance in his work? In a much more awe-

---

[1] ILLIMITABLE. *That which cannot be limited or bounded.*

[2] JEHOVAH-RAAH. *The Lord my Shepherd.*

some way, we are promised that if we seek our God, He will draw nigh unto us (James 4:8), be an ever-present help in time of need (Hebrews 4:16), and a Friend that never forsakes us (Hebrews 13:5). May we chase down His glories with the little measuring tapes He has given us—our minds—in the Scriptures!

that i may love him

In Matthew 22:37-38, Jesus commands, *"Thou shalt love the Lord thy God with all thy heart, and with all thy soul, and with all thy mind."* The massiveness of this principle goal, and my own failure to attain it, has often brought me to the question of the ages: How do I love Jesus Christ more?

Imagine for a minute that you have heard much about a person whose godly character traits you respect. If given the opportunity to spend time with her, you watch her interact with others and observe her life, and soon you can attest that she indeed vibrates with the power of Christ's love. The more you know of her virtues, the more your appreciation for her deepens. In a much greater way, the more time we spend with Christ our Savior through His Word, the more of His awing character we will see—and the greater our love for Him will grow. Thus, the answer to the question, "How do you love the Lord more?" is that you must know Him more. Because the truths of His character grip the redeemed heart in adoration, there is nothing else that can make us love God more, than knowing Him more personally. We must spend our life with Him, study His characteristics recorded from centuries past in the Scriptures—then our love for Christ will ever increase. Let it be our life's goal and driving purpose to *know* our Father more deeply, that we can *love* His name ever more passionately. *"I will love Thee, O LORD, my strength"* (Psalm 18:1).

that i may obey him

The Holy Scriptures disclose God's will and commands for our lives. I Thessalonians 4:2 communicates that His desire for us: "*Ye ought to walk and to please God, so ye would abound more and more. For ye know what commandments we gave you by the Lord Jesus. For this is the will of God, even your sanctification...that every one of you should know how to possess his vessel in sanctification and honour*" (I Thessalonians 4:1-3). The Lord desires for us to "*be conformed to the image of his Son*" (Romans 8:29); if our lives are to reflect Him, we must first "*study to shew [ourselves] approved unto God, a workman that needeth not to be ashamed, rightly dividing the word of truth*" (II Timothy 2:15). As the Bible reveals the image of God to us and instructs us in His will, it will convict and transform us into a "mini picture" of Jesus Christ, our Redeemer. Because this is the will of God, we must seek His Word as a habit, conforming ourselves to its standard by the work of the Spirit. "*The commandment is a lamp; and the law is light; and reproofs of instruction are the way of life*" (Proverbs 6:23).

> How can we walk in the way of God if we do not *know* His commands?

fountain of wisdom

Because the Scriptures are God's breath-inspired Word (Hebrews 4:12), they reveal His unfathomable wisdom. I love the apostle Paul's exclamation, "*O the depth of the riches both of the wisdom and knowledge of God! how unsearchable are his judgments, and his ways past finding out!*" (Romans 11:33) *Matthew Henry's Commentary on the Bible* notes of this glorious doxology, "Paul was well acquainted with the mysteries of the kingdom of God as ever any mere man was; and yet he confesses himself at a loss in the contemplation, and despairing to find the bottom, he humbly sits down at the brink, and adores its depth." As Paul did, we do well just to "sit down" at the ocean of God's wisdom and worship Him in its majestic magnitude!

No matter how phenomenal our eyesight might be, when we look down into the oceans' abyss,[3] we will never be able to see its floor. Similarly, only an insignificant portion of the chasms of God's wisdom can be penetrated by humanity. In the book of Job, the Lord asks questions which reveal the infinity of His mind, *"Where wast thou when I laid the foundations of the earth? declare, if thou hast understanding. Who hath laid the measures thereof, if thou knowest? or who hath stretched the line upon it? Whereupon are the foundations thereof fastened? or who laid the corner stone thereof?"* (Job 38) This is a beautiful passage to study and to bask in the magnitude of God's all-wise judgment. The most knowledgeable, brilliant mind is more ignorant than it is wise; the wisest theologian has only an infant's comprehension of the vast expanse of the Lord's intellect. *"For who hath known the mind of the Lord? or who hath been his counsellor? For of him, and through him, and to him, are all things: to whom be glory for ever. Amen"* (Romans 11:34-36).

> The word "*depth*" is applied in the Scrip-tures to anything vast and incomprehensible. As the abyss or the ocean is *unfathomable*, so the word comes to denote what words cannot express.
>
> (ALBERT BARNES)

James 1:5 says, *"If any of you lack wisdom, let him ask of God, that giveth to all men liberally, and upbraideth not; and it shall be*

---
[3] ABYSS. *A bottomless gulf.*

given him." It is incredible to think that God liberally offers His wisdom without respect of persons—to any who *ask*. We must implore the Lord to impart His wisdom to us, not for our own vain glory, but that we may understand His will, love Him more, and serve Him more passionately.

We are spiritually ignorant of so much because we have not humbled ourselves and simply asked the Lord for His wisdom. Proverbs pleads, *"Wisdom is the principal thing; therefore get wisdom: and with all thy getting get understanding"* (4:7). It continues, *"I [wisdom] lead in the way of righteousness, in the midst of the paths of judgment"* (Proverbs 8:20). Reverent fear of the Source of all wisom is the beginning of our own knowledge, as Proverbs 1:7 says, *"the fear of the LORD is the beginning of knowledge."* Christ is the One *"in whom are hid all the treasures of wisdom and knowledge"* (Colossians 2:4), and is called the *"wisdom of God"* (I Corinthians 1:24); therefore, as we diligently seek Christ in God through the Word, we will learn more of the mysteries of His will and truth.

The wisdom of the Bible is so inexhaustible that its truths could never be fully penetrated by our finite minds. The princi-

life passage

Pick a Bible passage to study each day of your life; every word contained in the Scriptures has so much meaning and can never be exhausted. I chose Psalms 119 as my "life passage" and am daily awed by its beauties as I study it.

ples contained in just one chapter could be gleaned throughout an entire lifetime! For example, Psalm twenty-seven opens, *"The LORD is my light and my salvation..."* There is so much to learn from this one statement; think of the first word: "the." It says *"the* LORD," not *"a* LORD," for we do not worship or follow more than one God (Exodus 20:3). There is only one Creator and one sovereign Lord above all, through all, and in all (Ephesians 4:6). Therefore, we never have to fear what would happen if He was "overruled" by another being. The Rock of our Salvation is supreme, He is our own hope, and by Him all things consist (Colossians 1:17). The next word is so precious to the believing heart: "LORD." The great I Am (Exodus 3:14) is our everlasting God and the Shepherd of His Sheep (I Peter 5:4); we are ever under His able care (Psalm 57:1), never beyond His love (Romans 8:35). The word "is" is the third person singular present of the verb "be," and from this we revel in the fact that our God, the *"Alpha and Omega, the beginning and the ending,"* is One *"which is, and which was, and which is to come"* (Revelation 1:8). The indescribable joy and comfort which this truth gives is awe-evoking—how can a finite mind wrap itself around the reality that God has always "been," and always will "be"? From these three opening words in Psalm 27, we can glean rich wisdom, and this is yet the beginning of all that can be expounded. Grab your Bible, a concordance, and a Bible dictionary—and start studying this precious passage as you pray for the Lord's teaching (Psalm 18:28).

a transforming flame

The more time we spend immersed in the Scriptures, studying and looking at Christ's face, the more His image will be mirrored in our own lives. II Corinthians 3:18 was penned so eloquently, *"We all, with open face beholding as in a glass the glory of the Lord, are changed into the same image from glory to glory, even as by the Spirit of the Lord."* Each time we come away from study of the Law of God, our lives will be imprinted a bit more by His holy facsimile[4]—probably not in our physical appearance, but in our heart and our countenance. When Moses dwelt in the presence of God's ineffable[5] glory for forty days, he came away with a bright shining countenance; it was so brilliant that he had to cover himself to approach the Israelites, for *"When Aaron and all the children of Israel saw Moses, behold, the skin of his face shone; and they were afraid to come nigh him"* (Exodus 34:30). Similarly, the Word of God is life-transforming, for it reveals to us His glory.

We must hide ourselves in the Scriptures and be devoted to seeking out His face through the mystery of the Gospel; this one thing—personal Scripture study at the feet of Christ—is one of the most vital keys to bearing a God-honoring, fruitful walk of Christianity. Until we are ready to humbly fall on our faces before the Lord and earnestly seek His Word, studying contexts, memorizing passages, talking and walking in the Truth—until then, we cannot expect to be filled with the knowledge of His will and the blessing He desires to bestow upon the diligent seeker of His face (James 4:8). May we each dedicate our entire lives to seeking out this "One Thing"!

preeminent life goal

"Seek ye the kingdom of God; and all these things shall be added unto you" (Luke 12:31). The most important habit we can make in our life is a daily time of dwelling in the Lord's presence, studying the depths of the Gospel revealed in His Word. What

---

[4] FACSIMILE. *An exact copy or likeness.*

[5] INEFFABLE. *Unspeakable; unutterable; that cannot be expressed in words.*

else in this world is worth committing all that we have—our very lives—to seeking out and being transformed by? A godly "Titus 2" mentor once shared with me, "I am very sure that everything I am comes from the time that I have spent with the Lord in those secret quiet times throughout my lifetime. As I look back over all the years with Him, I realize that purposing to keep this time with Him has been the one thing that has made my heart soft

> *source of wisdom*
> The entrance of thy words giveth light; it giveth understanding unto the simple.
> (PSALM 119:130)

to His conviction and commands." The choice we make in setting aside time each day to be with our Master will give Him the fertile ground in which to plant seeds of sanctification.[6] At the end of our life, when we look back over our walk with the Lord, we will know that the time spent with Him is what reaped any spiritual harvest in our lives. Jesus is the source of our strength, our "Vine" of life, for in John 15:4 He says, *Abide in me, and I in you. As the branch cannot bear fruit of itself, except it abide in the vine; no more can ye, except ye abide in Me.* We must dwell with Him day by day to be vessels of His strength and love.

Sitting at the feet of Jesus Christ in His Word is a thrilling journey—one which brings profound joy to the heart of one who loves Him. The more time I spend in the Scriptures, the more *"my heart standeth in awe of [God's] word"* (Psalm 119:161). It truly gives such joy and peace to my soul; something "new" constantly speaks to me through the Word in a precious and convicting way. When I feel discouraged over my failures, the Lord offers hope through His promises of faithfulness; when my

[6] SANCTIFICATION. *The at of God's grace by which the affections of men are purified or alienated from sin and the world, and exalted to a supreme love to God.*

heart is ready to burst with the joy of witnessing His provisions, it echoes Psalms' praises. Exhilaration fills my heart when I find similar promises throughout the Word—I love cross-referencing, writing down references in margins, jotting down how the Lord has used a certain verse to encourage or convict my heart, drawing lines to similar phrases, highlighting special portions, and memorizing verses. As my friend Grace Mally says in *Will Our Generation Speak?*, "Scripture is brimming with rich metaphors, comparisons, parallels, types,[7] and word pictures that give us a deeper understanding of the Gospel message."

One day as I was studying Proverbs, I noticed the word "righteousness" repeated many times, so I grabbed a colored pencil and began highlighting it, noticing the promises which followed commands to walk in righteousness. What a guide these truths are to our path. With excitement, it suddenly dawned on me that reading the Law of God is like doing a "word search"—only immeasurably more thrilling and valuable! Our Lord has given us an instructive "puzzle" to piece together throughout the rest of our lives, from the truths in His Word. It seems that the more I read, the more I find to learn about the God of my salvation, and the deeper my zeal grows to know Him. What a blessing it is to see God speak through it!

righteousness...

~Delivers from death

~Directs the way of the perfect

~Guides the upright

~Reaps a sure reward

~Tends to life

~Brings forth true words

~Is the way of life

(FROM PROVERBS 11-12)

---

[7] TYPE. *A symbol; a figure of something to come.*

hidden in the Word

Establishing a consistent, daily time to study Christ Jesus in His Word is a vital habit that must be established in our life, no matter what temporal sacrifice is required. There are many Bible study methods, schedules, and plans which can be incorporated in the time we spend with the Lord, but the goal remains the same: to know Him more deeply and personally. If you have not yet incorporated this time with Christ in your daily life, I encourage you to do whatever it requires to make this the number-one, highest priority in your day. Set aside a certain amount of time every day to seek God's face and ask for His wisdom as you read His Word. I want to challenge you to make a specific goal in this area, in order to form a life habit: during the next three weeks, set aside thirty minutes to an hour *every* day to spend with Jesus Christ in quietude, your Bible in hand. Even if that means waking up at an earlier hour or taking something out of your daily schedule; this is vitally important and will reap eternal fruit that you will never regret. I have challenged myself to similar goals and can testify that the time I spend with the Lord each day has been more spiritually deepening and more important than anything else I can do; it has been the *one thing* that has completely changed my life and filled me with the all-satisfying goodness of my Father day by day. Oftentimes we need this initial challenge to give ourself motivation to sit down long enough in quiet stillness to experience the vast wealth of the Scriptures. Once we "*taste and see that the LORD is good*" (Psalm 34:8), then the depths of His excellencies captivate us to *want* to seek Him daily. Because its wisdom is infinite, each day we will be amazed at the power of the Gospel to shape our lives into His precious image. "*The law of the LORD is perfect, converting the soul: the testimony of the LORD is sure, making wise the simple*" (Psalm 19:7).

One's devotional time with Christ should not be a list to "check off" or an uninteresting routine. Rather, it should be the highlight of our day—a thrilling quest to know the One Who died to "save a wretch like me," and learn how to please Him. If He truly is our greatest and deepest love, and we are living under the power of His Cross, then we will *delight* to be with Him! Our great joy should be found in seeking His Word for its gold and pearls of guidance. Seek to please the Lord through the way you spend time with Him; it does not always have to look the same, but you do need to have an or-

topical searches

∼Search for ways to praise the Lord in Psalms

∼Note references & blessings of "wisdom" in Proverbs

∼Highlight the names of Christ in John

∼Record the saving work of Jesus Christ in Romans

∼Underline the word "love" in I John

ganized, reachable goal and unwavering commitment for your daily devotions. The following are a few pointers which have been beneficial for me to remember in maintaining a solid time with the Lord.

∼ Make a disciplined habit to meet with Christ every day at the same time. Mornings often work well, when the mind is clear and focused (see Exodus 24:4, Judges 6:38, I Samuel 1:19, Psalm 5:3 and 59:16, Mark 1:35).

∼ Eliminate *all* distractions during this time, whether that means clearing off the table around you, moving books or to-do lists out of eyesight, turning music off, or avoiding unnecessary interruptions.

~Before opening your Bible, pray and ask for Christ's enlightenment to your mind (Psalm 119:144), for through Him alone can we understand His truth.

~If you choose to read through the Bible systematically, leave sticky notes with gleanings or questions. The next time you read through that passage, you may find that you are able to answer previous questions and the Lord impresses you with yet another aspect of its meaning. If a certain passage or book of the Bible has challenged you, study it for several months or memorize portions of it. Do not skip over portions you might tend to neglect; there is an important message in every book of the Bible.

~Interlink similar verses and notice reoccurring themes; for example, Exodus and Isaiah hold many parallel messages (compare Exodus 33:14 with Isaiah 43:2), as do Deuteronomy and Proverbs (note Deuteronomy 15:19 and Proverbs 3:9). A picture of a leaf from Frances Havergal's Bible inspired me to link similar phrases with thin lines like "railways," write down corresponding references, and connect collateral passages.

~As you read the Word, ask its Author how you can apply it to your life: are you living up to its standard?

~Find an effective method to record insights, God's attributes, things He lays on your heart, or special passages you encounter while you study.

~As you see God revealed each day in the Word, worship Him. Study His character, commands, Hebrew names and meanings, and His works.

~Establish a disciplined method of prayer during your daily quiet time.

⟡Memorize Scriptures which have convicted or blessed you, and review previously memorized passages daily.

Spending time with our Redeemer and studying His Word is such a joy and privilege, integral to the deepening of our knowledge and comprehension of the Gospel. We must invest discipline to establish this fundamental in our daily life. I encourage you to not let anything hinder the time you spend with your Maker every day. Though we all encounter busy days or times when we don't "feel" like sitting down quietly with the Lord, it is during these seasons that we most need to dwell in the peace of Christ and abide in Him, for His power to be manifest through us. What are the fleeting tasks and issues of this life in comparison to knowing the One we will spend all of eternity worshipping? Be committed to never let your time with Jesus slip by; let Him and His Word truly be the "apple of your eye"—your great longing, your highest pursuit, and your single-minded focus, as Proverbs 7:2 commands: *"Keep my command-ments, and live; and my law as the apple of thine eye."*

loving God's word...

How sweet are Thy Words ⟡
They are the rejoicing of my heart ⟡
Thy Law do I love ⟡
I love Thy Precepts ⟡
I rejoice at Thy Word ⟡
Thy Law is my delight ⟡

(FROM PSALM 119)

a lamp in darkness

David said, *"Thy word have I hid in mine heart, that I might not sin against Thee"* (Psalm 119:11). What better way to know God's will in our hearts for guidance—than by memorizing His life-transforming Word? God's people throughout the ages have found the Scriptures to be a powerful strength both for spiritual growth and in physical hardships. Countless missionaries and martyrs have found eternal hope in the Scripture which they memorized at an early age. The Lord uses His Word to convict, protect, and guide His people. How true is Isaiah 55:11, which says, *"So shall My word be that goeth forth out of My mouth: it shall not return unto Me void, but it shall accomplish that which I please."* The Scriptures are never void of power and always reap a result which honors the Lord.

When we take diligent heed to hide His Truth in our hearts, Christ will be able to use it mightily throughout our days. He has not promised us ease of life (Matthew 19:29, Luke 9:23), and the day may come when our Bibles are confiscated, or persecution and even martyrdom harshly stares us in the face; however, if God's Word is already tucked in our heart where it cannot be beaten out or taken away, the Lord can instruct and comfort our minds with it. Will you be prepared to refute evil with the truth of the Scriptures in your heart, whether you are being questioned about your Biblical convictions, or you are facing dark days of imprisonment in a concentration camp? Will you *"boldly say, The Lord is my helper, and I will not fear what man shall do unto me"* (Hebrews 13:6)? My dear friend, our generation is so caught up and fascinated by the latest gadgets and frivolous fads of the world—but these temporal things will not last in that final Judgment day. *"Our God is a consuming fire"* (Hebrews 12:29). We must realize that *"Heaven*

persecution

~Matthew 5:10

~Matthew 5:12

~Luke 21:12

~John 15:20

~Acts 7:5

~Romans 12:14

~II Corinthians 4:9

and earth shall pass away: but My words shall not pass away" (John 14:2). Will we leave behind all the trite things of dust and instead fill our minds with what will last through all ages and fiery trials—the Word of our God (Isaiah 40:8)? May we invest, with unwavering penetrating focus, in the Scriptures now while the opportunity is before us, as Ecclesiastes 12:1 instructs, *"Remember now thy Creator in the days of thy youth, while the evil days come not, nor the years draw nigh, when thou shalt say, I have no pleasure in them."*

memory passages
Ruth 1:16-17 ∽
Psalm 16, 42, 63, 119, 139 ∽
Isaiah 6, 12, 42, 53 ∽
Daniel 2:20-23, 9 ∽
John 15 & 17 ∽
Romans 5 & 12 ∽
I Corinthians 13 ∽
II Corinthians 4 ∽
Colossians 3 ∽
I Thessalonians 5:14-28 ∽
Galatians 5:13-22 ∽
Philippians 1, 2, 3, & 4 ∽
Ephesians 3:14-21 & 5 ∽
I Peter 1:3-21 & 2 ∽
(SAMPLE IDEAS)

unwavering diligence

Scripture memory requires a commitment of time and energy, but the compensation far exceeds that investment. I have to admit that in the past, I have been discouraged by the effort that this discipline involves; however, that attitude was only an unfortunate indicator of how much my spiritual walk lacked. Having now made Scripture memory a priority in my journey, the Lord has used it as a potent tool in my life. This last year, by God's enabling grace, I was able to memorize more than at any previous time in my life. I can confidently proclaim the power of Scripture memory and encourage you to experience its blessings for yourself! If you have never diligently memorized

God's Word before, begin by establishing a reachable goal of memorizing one or two verses a week. You will soon find that as you commit yourself to this objective and flood your mind with God's truth, your walk with Him will be reenforced.

Each individual will have an unique method through which they can most effectively memorize; whether it be by verbal repetition, writing the passage repeatedly, listening to it audibly, or arranging the verses to a musical tune, learn what works best for your mind to memorize Scripture.

Personally, as I study the Word I write down passages that have particularly rich teaching on a "Scripture Memory To-Do List"; therefore, I always have a list of verses to memorize. I then add these chapters of the audio Bible to a folder and frequently listen to them throughout the day as I work, so that by this repetition, they become familiar to my mind. Thus, when I am ready to choose a new portion to memorize each week, I already have a head-start on memorizing it. Each morning during my daily quiet time I audibly say or write each verse repeatedly until I can remember it. I have also found that hanging the passages I am memorizing in a predominate area—on a bathroom mirror, the kitchen window, beside a desk or bed—helps keep the verses available for meditation.

When the Scriptures are hidden in our hearts, the Lord is able to convict us and bring Truth to mind for comfort or guidance in time of need. *"Thy word is a lamp unto my feet, and a light unto my path"* (Psalm 119:105). I have been blessed many times as the Lord has convicted or led me through verses previously memorized. Even if you have a hard time remembering passages you have worked on, remind yourself that God's Word never returns void (Isaiah 55:11). One particular passage that I memorized was quite a challenge for me, and I remember wondering how it would benefit me later in life, if I could not even recite it while I studied it daily. However, a few nights later my doubts were quieted when those very verses came to mind and flowed on effortlessly. In this way, the Lord washed my mind with His beautiful Words. Truly, our time is never unwisely spent in God's Law, for our lives need to be saturated in His truth, that we may be trained to counter the wickedness of our own hearts. Our prayer must be, as we memorize the Word of God, *"Order my steps in Thy word: and let not any iniquity have dominion over me"* (Psalm 119:133).

accountability & review

A vital aid in committing Scripture to memory is establishing godly accountability. I know that I am much weaker in my diligence to memorize if I do not have this; therefore, I regularly ask a family member or friend to be my "accountability partner" for two or three months, and we together purpose to memorize a certain number of verses weekly. During that time, we recite our passages to one another every two weeks on the phone. It is motivating and refreshing to keep

titles of God's word...

Oracles of God ∽

Sharper than Two-Edged Sword ∽

Sweeter than honey ∽

Bread from Mouth of God ∽

Royal Law ∽

Milk for Newborn Babes ∽

Schoolmaster ∽

Amour of Righteousness ∽

Sword of the Spirit ∽

(FIND THE SCRIPTURE SOURCE!)

one another accountable in Scripture memory, and these conversations are also an opportunity to glorify Christ by praying for one another and speaking of God's righteousness. *"I am a companion of all them that fear thee, and of them that keep thy precepts"* (Psalm 119:63). Malachi 3:16 says, *"They that feared the LORD spake often one to another: and the LORD hearkened, and heard it, and a book of remembrance was written before Him for them that feared the LORD, and that thought upon His name."* I would encourage you to make yourself accountable to your parents, siblings, or a godly friend in your memorization goal; this is one of the most effective ways to keep yourself diligent to hide God's Word in your heart. *"I will speak of the glorious honour of Thy majesty, and of Thy wondrous works"* (Psalm 145:5).

Scripture memory is an on-going life work, and previously memorized passages must be reviewed frequently—for they are prone to fade from memory if not refreshed. Establishing a routine of review during your regular Bible times may be most effective for fitting this into your schedule. I know of some who write each memorized passage on an index card and review a few of these cards daily. The method that has worked for me has been to print out all the passages I have memorized, and daily I recite a few pages' worth of verses; I also continue to listen to the audio Bible chapters. There are many ways to review Scripture, so I encourage you to find an arrangement which works for you and then construct it in your daily schedule.

kindling a flame

It is a great joy to share with others the blessing we find in seeing our Redeemer in the Scriptures. One summer, my sister and I took a challenge together, which encouraged us to read the Bible for at least fifteen minutes every day, memorize a minimum of one verse each week, and recite to an accountability partner regularly. We were very excited about this pursuit, so we invited friends to do it as well—and since the goal of reading and memorizing God's Word is profitable for anyone, not just young ladies, we invited our brothers to join us! We were thrilled when they decided to do it as well, and we printed individual charts for each of us to record the amount of time daily spent in the Word and memorized passages. It was such a joy to pursue God's Word all summer together, encouraging one another in the Lord and working on our memorization projects together. The fellowship we each had with our respective accountability partners also sharpened us in the Lord, as Proverbs 27:17 says, *"Iron sharpeneth iron; so a man sharpeneth the countenance of his friend."* At the end of the challenge, my sister and I made a special meal and dessert for our brothers as a "congratulation" for completing the challenge.

That summer of seeking the Lord and working towards Scripture memory goals with one another was so special. We eagerly look forward to doing this "pursuit" together annually.

Let the joy you find in God's Word flow from your life to everyone around you; encourage others to taste of God's greatness with you, so that together you may proclaim, *"How sweet are Thy words unto my taste! yea, sweeter than honey to my mouth!"* (Psalm 119:103) Make

Join me for the
autumn *Quest!*
Dates: _____

QUEST RULES
- Spend at least 15 minutes each day with the Lord
- Memorize at least 1 Bible verse a week and recite it to your accountability partner.
- Call your accountability partner every two weeks to recite to one another and share prayer requests.

Verses Memorized	Sunday	Monday	Tuesday	Wednesday	Thursday	Friday	Saturday	Total Time

fun "Bible mysteries" and quizzes for your brothers and sisters which will spur their deeper study of the Scriptures. For example, give your brothers a brick and ask them, "I built a great wall with one hand, while holding a weapon in the other! Who am I?" (Nehemiah 4:17) Or, "Are you as good at shooting your slingshot as I am? Though I am left-handed, I am so practiced in shooting that I could shoot and not miss within a hair's breadth." (Judges 20:16) Cut out a piece of purple linen and give it to your sisters with the mystery, "The Lord opened my heart and caused me to worship Him with joy. I housed a powerful apostle of Christ and enjoyed working diligently with my hands." (Acts 16:14, 40) The ideas are endless and will prompt your own deeper study of the Word.

> Take good heed therefore unto yourselves, that ye *love* the LORD your God.
>
> (JOSHUA 24:13-14)

Encourage your siblings and friends to make daily devotions, prayer, and Scripture memory a solid commitment at a young age. Host a Bible reading challenge and decorate colorful little invitations and charts for a "Bible quest"; you can even offer prizes or goodies for those who complete it. Challenge young friends at church to memorize five verses in two weeks with you, and then have a little gathering and recite to one another. It is so exciting to seek the Lord as a Body of Christ (Ephesians 4:12). Your motivation and example, especially to those younger than yourself, can be used by the Lord as a powerful tool in other young lives, and countless others with whom they come in contact. As *"the salt of the earth"* (Matthew 5:13), it should be our desire to create in others a thirst to know the Lord God better and to be satisfied with His Living Water, which alone can quench one's spiritual thirst (John 7:38).

In this generation, zeal for God's Word and His truth is much lacking—but oh, so needed (read Numbers 25:7-13 to see God's blessings upon those who stand zealously for truth). May we ardently pursue—and proclaim—the Gospel found in the Scriptures to the dying world around us (Ephesians 6:12), asking the Lord to give us a bold eagerness to share His Law with others. David unabashedly said, *"I will speak of Thy testimonies also before kings, and will not be ashamed"* (Psalm 119:46). We must fearlessly proclaim His Word with love, desiring that all would believe unto salvation (Romans 10:10). I Peter 3:15 commands us to *"be ready always to give an answer to every man that asketh you a reason of the hope that is in you with meekness and fear."* Do not be ashamed to take a bold and zealous stand for Truth, for all who scoff at it will one day bow the knee to its Author, and will be judged by it for his sins—if he has not first come to Christ for mercy and redemption (Romans 14:11). Proverbs 13:13 says, *"Whoso despiseth the word shall be destroyed: but he that feareth the commandment shall be rewarded."* The Scriptures can be our tool in witnessing to those who are lost, by showing them their broken state using God's standard of the ten commandments (Exodus 20), explaining the necessary punishment for such transgression against a holy Judge, and then pointing them to the only hope of salvation through the sacrifice of God's Son, Jesus Christ—offered freely to all that *"call upon the name of the Lord"* (Romans 10:13). As we earnestly tell others of Christ, the coming Judgement, and His Word, may we do so with genuine, Christ-exalting concern, meekness, and grace.

signs of remembrance

Throughout the Scriptures, the Lord tells us the importance of firmly binding His law to our hearts and lives. In Numbers 15:38, God commanded the Israelites to bind blue tassels on their garments, *"that ye may remember, and do all my commandments, and be holy unto your God."* In Deuteronomy 11:18, He told His people: *"Therefore shall ye lay up these My words in your heart and in your soul, and bind them for a sign upon your hand, that they may be as frontlets between your eyes."* His law was to be "etched" upon their hands, and as visible as a band worn around the forehead! Proverbs 7:2-3 gives a graphic image of how the Scriptures should be bound to our fingers and written on the "table" of our heart as a continual reminder and guide. Why is this so important to our God and why does He emphasize it so frequently?

bind them continually upon thine heart, and tie them about thy neck. For the commandment is a lamp; and the law is light.

(PROVERBS 6:21,23)

"We know that we are of God, and the whole world lieth in wickedness" (I John 5:19). We abide in a sin-soaked culture where wickedness abounds and is widely promoted by those who actively seek to defy God; because of these ungodly surroundings, our input of God's truth must exceed our absorption of the world's deadly lies. Without His revelation, we would walk in the obscurity of our own sin and superstition (Hosea 4:6). Thus, Deuteronomy 4:9 warns, *"Take heed to thyself, and keep thy soul diligently, lest thou forget the things which thine eyes have seen."* Our Maker knows that we are desperately prone to forget His commands and marvelous works, and this is the first step of our faith's

deterioration. In Psalm 78:10-11 we read about the disobedience of the Israelites when *"they kept not the covenant of God,
and refused to walk in His law, and forgat His works, and His wonders that He had shewed them."* We tread dangerous waters if we
forget God's commands and His merciful works on our behalf,
for *"where there is no vision, the people perish: but he that keepeth the
law, happy is he"* (Proverbs 29:18).

Therefore, we must firmly plant God's law in our hearts
and lives so that it penetrates our very being and offers guidance
in every step. We are presented with many choices in which we
can bind the Scriptures before our eyes and mind, in order to
refute sin's dominion in our life. Everything that surrounds us
and enters our minds can be mementos of His Word. Therefore
at every turn, we should seek to place it in front of our eyes,
mind, and heart.

There are many practical ways to pour the Scriptures into
our lives; aspire to find every possible way to put the law of God before your eyes. In so doing, the Holy Spirit will convict you as you abide in Him. Decorate your home with beautiful Scriptural artwork—cross-stitched or embroidered designs, scenic photos, paintings,

May *God's word* be our...

~Meditation (Psalm 119:97)

~Joy (Jeremiah 15:16)

~Peace (Psalms119:165)

~Shield (Proverbs 30:5)

~Heritage (Psalm 119:111)

~Righteousness (Psalm 119:172)

or other forms of God-glorifying art. Frequently print memory
verses or passages that have blessed you and then place them
around your home. You can put a little box beside your bed or
desk containing verses written on index cards; each morning,

pick a card and meditate on that passage throughout the day. Write special verses down for this collection during your daily Bible time.

Colossians 3:16 says, *"Let the word of Christ dwell in you richly in all wisdom; teaching and admonishing one another in psalms and hymns and spiritual songs, singing with grace in your hearts to the Lord."* The Word of God should always be on our lips; singing its words (Psalm 96:2) brings to our mind His goodness and truth (Psalm 101:1). Scriptures and Psalms arranged to music is an effective way to saturate ourselves with God's wisdom throughout our waking hours, by both listening to and singing—*"making melody in your heart to the Lord"* (Ephesians 5:19).

I frequently wash my mind by listening to recorded Scriptures throughout the day. *"Cleanse your hands, ye sinners; and purify your hearts, ye double minded"* (James 4:8). Hearing the Word of God purifies and instructs me in the righteous path of the Lord. Similarly, Biblical, Christ-honoring sermons inspire spiritual growth; with your authority's permission and support, listen to a series of sermons or theological teachings often—daily, if possible. Always listen discerningly, comparing what is taught with the solid truth of God's Word. Listening to Scriptural expositions has powerfully deepened my own spiritual walk; I usually do this while I work, exercise, or travel.

I love to write verses I am currently memorizing on little pieces of paper and include those in letters, or hand them to those who are going through difficult times. (Not only does this share the precious blessings of God's Word with others, but it also helps me memorize the passage.) There are many ways to share the Bible with others; take your neighbors fresh-baked bread with a Scripture verse written on top; send a card to a friend who is ill with a special Promise; give your cashier

a beautifully-written verse on a little card. May we be unwavering in our commitment to share God's Word, praying as the
disciples did in Acts 4:31 for greater boldness. II Timothy 1:12
says, *"I am not ashamed: for I know whom I have believed, and am
persuaded that He is able to keep that which I have committed unto
Him against that day."* The Gospel reveals the only way of eternal
life, therefore, since God *"hast given a banner to them that fear
[Him], that it may be displayed because of the truth"* (Psalm 60:4),
may we never waver to hold it highly!

it is our life

In Deuteronomy 6:4, Moses declared the greatest command for all people—*"Thou shalt love the LORD Thy God with
all thine heart, and with all thy soul, and with all thy might."* He
continued with the exhortation, *"these words, which I command
thee this day, shall be in thine heart: and thou shalt teach them diligently unto thy children, and shalt talk of them when thou sittest in
thine house, and when thou walkest by the way, and when thou liest
down, and when thou risest up."* As we love the Lord our God,
we are commanded to keep His Word on our heart. We are
further instructed to teach it diligently to our children as we
sit, walk, lie down, and arise up again. Seeking out this One
Thing—the Gospel of Christ—is of utmost importance, for
one day we will be called to pass down this life-changing Story
to our children, grandchildren, and great-grandchildren (Deuteronomy 4:9). In our youth is the time to seek out the Lord's
face through rigorous study of His Word, for our responsibilities now are fewer than they will be in the future. Our love for
Christ must be fueled daily by the flame of His Word, that our
fire for Him will be kindled strong and bright—and in turn,
our lives will be a spark of encouragement to the next genera-

tion, that they too faithfully love and serve the Lord God, if He so tarries.

Deuteronomy 32:46-7 says, *"Set your hearts unto all the words which I testify among you,"* and continues—*"for it is not a vain thing for you; because it is your life."* The Word is our very life! This is one of the most important investments we can make during our time on earth; therefore, in it let us seek to know the One Who redeemed us at such an infinite cost—that our hearts would be wholly captivated by His glorious love. *"The God of our Lord Jesus Christ, the Father of glory, may give unto you the spirit of wisdom and revelation in the knowledge of Him"* (Ephesians 1:17).

"Nowhere does Jehovah-Jesus appear to the spiritu-al, believing mind so *exalted* as when He stoops, so *glorious* as when in eclipse, so *holy* as when bearing sin, so *loving* as when enduring its punishment, so *triumphant* as when vanquished upon the Cross!"

octavius winslow

"The man who can get believers

to *pray* would, under God,

usher in the greatest revival

that the world has ever known.

There is *no* fault in God.

He is able."

leonard ravenhill

THREE

o n **bent knees**

Lying on my back in the itchy grass, I gazed up at the epic panorama of stars blanketed far above. The heavens' chasm inundated[1] with mystery and luminescing glory. Occasionally, a shooting star caused me to start in amazement; no wonder many have been fascinated by the heavens' many marvels! Although approximately six thousand stars are visible to the human eye, there are more than 100,000,000,000 fantastically unique stars in our galaxy alone. Hinting at the awing revelations of modern astronomy, I Corinthians 15:41 speaks of this vault of glory: *"There is one glory of the sun, and another glory of the moon, and another glory of the stars: for one star differeth from another star in glory."* Billions of galaxies, besides the one in which we live, were stretched out *"like a curtain"* (Psalm 104:2) by God's simple commanding word: *"He made the stars also"* (Genesis 1:16). Imagine the pleasure the Lord had in creating the expanse of the firmament, simply to reveal to man a glimpse of His measureless, immortal power!

As I stared into the sky's depths and thought of my own

---

[1] INUNDATE. *To overflow; to deluge.*

trifling size in comparison, I felt awed by the thought that the Creator of this universe is the One Who beckons me to come boldly to His throne, *"that we may obtain mercy, and find grace to help in time of need"* (Hebrews 4:16). This magnificent Sovereign is my heavenly Father Who comforts me in the night watches when my heart is heavy, Who offers a glow of hope through His unfailing promises, Who blesses my heart through the Gospel truths until it cannot hold any more, Who created these innumerable galaxies—and *He delights* in my prayers and stoops to hear every whispered plea! This is an incredible thought.

gift of prayer

Prayer is the line of communication that we have been given with the great Creator of all things, Who cannot even fit into the worlds He created, and Whose sustaining presence maneuvers the smallest atom. Have you realized the inconceivable privilege of being able to pray to such a God? This is the Jehovah who invites, *"call upon Me in the day of trouble: I will deliver thee"* (Psalm 50:15), and promises, *"call unto Me, and I will answer thee, and shew thee great and mighty things, which thou knowest not"* (Jeremiah 33:3). What would it be like, if the Lord created this world, gave humans a commission of dominion, and sent a wondrous Mediator for man's redemption—yet gave no way of direct communication with Himself? We would never be able to offer our praises to Him for His great mercies toward us, or witness His goodness in answering prayer. What a blessing it is to have a prayer-hearing God Who delights in hearing and answering our supplications. What idol, however earnestly besought, will hear or answer prayers? The privilege we have been given to be able to commune with our Father is a phenomenal reality.

The mercy of our holy God is revealed in the gift of prayer.

Picture the reality of man's state before His throne: here is one who has spent years in disgusting squalor,[2] and yet he dares to drag himself into the holy presence of the highest of all Monarchs, Who is seated on His jeweled throne. *"He that sat was to look upon like a jasper and a sardine stone: and there was a rainbow round about the throne, in sight like unto an emerald"* (Revelation 4:3). We are sinful creatures, and though our petitions are directed by the Holy Spirit (Romans 8:26), they are mixed with our iniquity and pride. Everything we do, even in obedience to the Lord, is tainted[3] by our own filth. Sometimes we even pray to be seen by others as a spiritual person—the depth of our prideful self-righteousness is astounding! However, the great mercy of God is that there is *"therefore now no condemnation to them which are in Christ Jesus"* (Romans 8:1) when we walk into His holy presence through prayer—for our Deliverer (Romans 11:26) has washed away our filth at the price of His own blood (Revelation 1:5). No longer is there a veil to hide God's throne from us, for Jesus' atonement has broken down the separating wall of our sin (Ephesians 2:14). This should cause our hearts to bow in utter worship and adoration for our King, for He has given such merciful admittance to the greatest of all throne rooms.

> The *fruit* we produce as a Christian— the life we produce as Christians— is directly related to *prayer.*
> (D.A. CARSON)

Every child of God has welcomed entrance through prayer, because Jesus *"hath made us kings and priests unto God and His Father; to Him be glory and dominion for ever and ever"* (Revelation 1:6).

---

[2] SQUALOR. *Foulness; filthiness.*

[3] TAINTED. *Infected; corrupted; stained.*

In the Old Testament, only blemish-free Levite priests could approach God; however, through our Advocate (I John 2:1), every believer is now accounted a "priest," and can therefore come directly to the Lord in prayer (Hebrews 4:14). Prayer shows us great things about the character of our Lord, for He is willing to stoop to hear our prayers and is eager to bestow His gifts of grace like a mighty flowing river. Realizing that the Son of God purchased for us the privilege of prayer and *"He ever liveth to make intercession"* (Hebrews 7:25), how can we neglect a gift so glorious? *"The prayer of the upright is His delight"* (Proverbs 15:8).

where is the power

We as mortal humans possess no ability to do good, to please God, or to attain spiritual victory—outside of the power of Jesus Christ. If there are battles to be fought or enemies to vanquish, it only will be accomplished through vigilant supplication at the throne of grace. Colossians 2:10 reminds us, *"Ye are complete in Him, which is the head of all principality and power."* Just as a body cannot do anything without the head, so are we utterly powerless without Christ, our spiritual "head" (Ephesians 4:15). How we desperately need to constantly realize our own weakness and limitation, that we would be driven further to our knees before our gracious Lord!

> We must not come with doubtful minds; we must know that God is much more *ready to give* than we are to receive.
> (MARTYN-LLOYD JONES)

Any spiritual growth and any fruitfulness in our lives or the Church is only to be achieved through prevailing, believing prayer. We must be deeply committed to prayer, as we find the early church leaders in Acts 6:4, who said, *"we will give ourselves continually to prayer, and to the ministry of the word."* The overflowing blessing of their dedication to prayer and ministry is seen through the power of the early Christian church and its countless conversions: *"The word of God increased; and the number of the disciples multiplied in Jerusalem greatly; and a great company of the priests were obedient to the faith"* (Acts 6:7). God's ability or desire to work in His people has not diminished since this vibrant time of the early Church's growth; He delights in giving good and perfect gifts to those who ask in faith (Luke 11:13). Could it be that the lack of power today in our lives, ministries, churches, and evangelism, is a result of our lack of dependence on Him? Because we are not wholly reliant on the provision of our head, Christ Jesus? Because we are not found on our knees in prayer?

Martin Luther once wrote, "I have so much business I cannot get on without spending three hours daily in prayer." The impact that so many preachers, theologians, and men and women of God have had throughout the history of the Church is solely based on their personal prayer time. "No man is greater than his prayer life," observed Leonard Ravenhill. This is the thermometer from which we can take the power of one's life, for it is the hidden hours spent before God's throne that produces a strong, fruit-bearing Christian walk. These private, faithful habits of devotion to the Lord establish strong foundations, bold testimonies, and rich legacies for future generations to build upon.

In his orphanage ministry, George Mueller trusted God for all monetary provisions through prayer. Instead of begging others for support, he went to his knees and asked his heavenly Father for needed resources. Daily, he prayed for several hours; once he testified, "I live in the spirit of prayer, I pray as I walk, when I lie down, and when I rise; the answers are always coming. Tens of thousands of times have my prayers been answered. When once I am persuaded a thing is right, I go on praying for it until the end comes. I never give up." Never was this man failed by God, for as Mueller trusted for provision, the Lord would speak to His people and prompt them to contribute in the needed form and time. The equivalent of millions of dollars were provided as answers to prayer throughout this faith-based ministry. George Mueller's seventy-two years of trust in the Lord inspire us today to a deeper walk of prayer.

where is the boldness

We often fail to pray for our Lord's perfect provision because of a lack of faith—however, there is no cause for doubt, when we know our God creates and moves mountains with one word! *"Ah Lord GOD! behold, Thou hast made the heaven and the earth by Thy great power and stretched out arm, and there is nothing too hard for Thee"* (Jeremiah 32:17). Where is our boldness at His throne? *"If ye shall ask any thing in My name, I will do it"* (John 14:14), we are promised. The example of Elijah shows a humble yet bold man of prayer (James 5:17-18); in I Kings 18:38, he confidently asked the Lord to magnify Himself through consuming a wettened sacrifice before the disobedient Israelites. This is God's prompt answer—*"The fire of the LORD fell, and consumed the burnt sacrifice, and the wood, and the stones, and the dust, and licked up the water that was in the trench."* That would have been an awe-striking event to witness! As a result of Elijah's prayer and God's provision, *"when all the people saw it, they fell on their faces: and they said, The LORD, He is the God."* Elijah was not a "super-spiritual" man; he simply trusted God and depended on Him in prayer, and the result was powerful and nation-wide revival. Leonard Ravenhill notes in his book, *Why Revival Tarries,*

"Elijah made it as difficult as he could for the Lord. He wanted fire, but yet he soaked the sacrifice with water! God loves such holy boldness in our prayers (Psalm 2:8)." We are to come before God's throne in boldness and faith, knowing that He keeps His promises and desires in our dependency on Him. When we do not take hold of the promises given to every believer in God's Word (II Peter 1:4), we show a lack of faith in the character and ability of our good Father, Who delights in working mighty wonders for our good (Daniel 4:3).

> We, going up into the mount of prayer, away from the world, *alone with God*, catch the rays of His glory... We then reflect out on the world the moral glory of God from 'glory to glory,' each new time of communion with Him catching something new of His *glory to reflect.*
> (R.A. TORREY)

As the Source of all created things, our Lord is not a stingy giver; He is eager to bestow abundant gifts. God has not only covenanted to do His people good, but also He has done so in great joy and anticipation. In Jeremiah 32:41 He proclaims, *"Yea, I will rejoice over them to do them good, and I will plant them in this land assuredly with My whole heart and with My whole soul."* The Lord eagerly anticipates every opportunity He can do good for His children; He does not begrudge their prayers or resent their dependency on Him. Instead, He welcomes both with great joy. This fact has encouraged me so greatly—just to think that my heavenly Father is waiting to hear my pleas for help and for grace.

In Luke 10:2, when Christ spoke to His disciples on the importance of prayer, He noted, *"The harvest truly is great, but the laborers are few."* Then, as the Lord of Heaven and earth, He commanded them to *"pray ye therefore the Lord of the harvest, that He would send forth laborers into His harvest."* It is made so clear that we, as God's people, have a calling and responsibility to pray. He delights in receiving our every prayer of faith and always answers in His perfect timing and sovereign plan. I John 5:14 says, *"This is the confidence that we have in Him, that, if we ask anything according to His will, He heareth us."* Therefore, I Peter 4:7 solemnly commands us, *"The end of all things is at hand: be ye therefore sober, and watch unto prayer."*

poured at his feet

Our Savior Jesus Christ led the ultimate life of prayer. If anyone has ever served others to the point of exhaustion, Jesus did—as day in and day out, He taught, served, and healed the impoverished masses. However, though *"all the city was gathered together at the door,"* Mark 1:35 records that our Lord arose early in the morning to commune with His heavenly Father in solitude. He slipped away from the noise and bustle of the multitudes—not to rest, not to go fishing—but to be with His God in prayer. We tend to "slip away" to do the things we enjoy most; do we frequently escape from the constant distractions of this world to abide in our Savior's strengthening presence? If the incarnate Son of God, Who possessed power without measure, gleaned guidance through prayer, how much more so are we, who are weak and prone to sin, in need of it? How much more should we look to the Lord in prayer?

We must regularly sit at the feet of our Lord, pouring out our heart, desires, needs, and soul (Hebrews 4:16), gleaning from His life-giving power. *I don't need a specific time to pray every day, because I pray all of the time*—is just an excuse; constant communion is of course our ultimate goal, but even then we must set aside time to spend alone at the feet of our Lord. We are not greater than Christ, Who frequently went into solitude to pray (Matthew 14:23).

exemplary prayer

Can you imagine what it would have been like to behold the Son of God communing with His Father? It must have been a moving scene to witness this Man of prayer pouring Himself out before God. We find His disciples struck by its power and imploring, *"Lord, teach us to pray"* (Luke 11:1). It is a privilege to know His response to this query, which is found in Matthew 6:9-13. Jesus Christ's model prayer unfolds,

> *"Our Father which art in Heaven, Hallowed be Thy name."*

First, we notice the title of "Father"; in prayer, we approach One Who is precious to us and Whose love for us supersedes anything we can ever imagine (Romans 8:39). *"Because ye are sons, God hath sent forth the Spirit of His Son into your hearts, crying, Abba, Father"* (Galatians 4:6). He cares about us more than any human father can, yet He also stands in authority and rulership. As His adopted child (Romans 8:15), we approach God with no merit of our own, yet clothed with the righteousness of His Son, Jesus Christ. Therefore, we come to the throne with great humility, in the name of our Intercessor (Hebrews 4:14-16).

Second, note Christ's act in sanctifying and consecrating His Father's name. The name of a person represents

thy name's sake
~I Samuel 12:22
~Psalm 23:3
~Psalm 25:11
~Psalm 106:8
~Psalm 143:11
~Isaiah 66:5
~Matthew 19:29
~Mark 13:13

his character and his value; therefore, the name of our Lord is to be adored and highly revered, lifted up and exalted *"above the heavens...above all the earth"* (Psalm 57:11)—for it reflects His holiness, righteousness, and truth. Jesus taught in John 15:16, *"Ye have not chosen me, but I have chosen you, and ordained you, that ye should go and bring forth fruit, and that your fruit should remain: that whatsoever ye shall ask of the Father in My name, He may give it you."* Here we are commanded to pray in the name of Jesus Christ our Mediator, Whose character and value mirrors His Father's. In this Name alone can we access God's great and noble throne, because He is the One Who redeemed and now forever intercedes for us. Through His blood we are adopted as God's sons (I John 3:1). *"Because ye are sons, God hath sent forth the Spirit of His Son into your hearts, crying, Abba, Father. Wherefore thou art no more a servant, but a son; and if a son, then an heir of God through Christ"* (Galatians 4:6). Because we are not righteous, we can only commune with God through

Christ's prayers recorded in the Bible are beautiful passages to memorize and to model our prayers after.
Matthew 11:24-27 ∽
Luke 10:21-22 ∽
John 11:41-42 ∽
John 17 ∽

His holy Son, Whose work on the Cross purchased our redemption and breached the gap which separated us, in our sin, from the Lord in His holiness. As a dear mentor pointed out to me, "In using the name of Christ in our prayers, it is far more than merely adding His name at the end of what we request. Using His name is to come before the Father in His holiness, through His redemption."

We approach the Lord in the great Name of His Son in

16

reverence, submission, and awe, yet at the same time, with confident faith in His goodness and mercy toward us through Christ. As Hebrews 4:16 commands, *"Let us therefore come boldly unto the throne of grace, that we may obtain mercy, and find grace to help in time of need."*

"Thy Kingdom come.
Thy will be done in earth, as it is in Heaven."

Through this acknowledgement, we show our allegiance to God and His supreme will. Submission to our Father is integral; He knows far more than we can ever imagine and His plan is always best (Romans 8:28); He *"is able to do exceeding abundantly above all that we ask or think"* (Ephesians 3:20). We find the paramount example of submission in Jesus Himself, Who was tested and proven faultless as He faced the rejection of His Father on behalf of His people (Matthew 26:42). Christ's last prayer on the mount of Olives was one for deliverance (Matthew 26:39); however, it was not granted, so that our prayers for eternal salvation can be. Does this reality not bring you to your knees in humbled reverence and submission to your Father and glorious King? Let our greatest desire in prayer be that our Lord performs His will in accordance with His unparalleled plan, through our lives and in Christ's body (Ephesians 4:12).

"Give us this day our daily bread."

In asking our Father for our "daily bread," we imply our dependence on God for the provision of our needs. *John Wesley's Explanatory Notes on the Whole Bible* comments that "our daily bread" includes "all things needful for our souls and bodies: not only the meat that perisheth, but the sacramental bread, and thy grace, the food which endureth to everlasting life." God sustains our every physical and spiritual need, as Psalm 145:15 says, *"The eyes of all wait upon Thee; and Thou givest them their meat in due season."* Therefore, we recognize that He is our Provider and Sustainer, and that apart from Him, we have no hope of existence.

In entreating the Lord for our daily provisions, first, we might ask, *What is my need for this day?* God's commands give us a glimpse of our true needs: *"Be not conformed to this world: but be ye transformed by the renewing of your mind, that ye may prove what is that good, and acceptable, and perfect, will of God"* (Romans 12:2). The Lord's desire for our lives is that we would be transformed into His image. Herein, we see *this* should be the object of our petitions: to implore God to grant grace for the renewal of our mind and life. *"Delight thyself also in the LORD; and He shall give thee the desires of thine heart"* (Psalm 37:4). When we take our eyes away from ourselves and realize God's over-arching plan, our *needs*—and greatest desires—become *God's* will, and this He is well-pleased to perform.

> We have a glorious *mediator*, Who has prepared the way, that our prayers may be heard consistently with the honour of God's justice and majesty.
> (JONATHAN EDWARDS)

Thus, when we daily pray, "Give us this day our daily bread," instead of our "need" being our fleeting desire or wish of the day, it becomes a plea for greater humility, submission, love, compassion, discipline, purity—the fruits of the Spirit (Galatians 5:22 and Ephesians 5:9). This is not to say that our Father does not desire to hear us ask for provision for our more "physical" needs, for He is pleased that we bring every request before Him if we do so in submission—desiring *His will* and glory. James 4:3 says, *"Ye ask, and receive not, because ye ask amiss, that ye may consume it upon your lusts."* We must recognize that He is our provider, we intake every breath by His power, and that every good thing *"cometh down from the Father of lights"* (James 1:17).

"And forgive us our debts, as we forgive our debtors."

Let us come to this portion of prayer with humble evaluation and trepidation, for if we are knowingly harboring bitterness or lack of forgiveness against another, how can we ask God to forgive our own vast transgressions? In Matthew eighteen, an analogy is given of our sin before our righteous Judge: a servant owing an astronomical amount of money to a king begged for mercy so that he might have time to pay off his obligation, though there was no earthly way he could ever do so. The *"lord of that servant was moved with compassion, and loosed him, and forgave him the debt"* (Matthew 18:27). What compassion this king demonstrated in alleviating the modern equivalent of billions of dollars; however, we immediately see this servant's odious lack of forgiveness toward another and wonder at his harshness: *"The same servant went out, and found one of his fellowservants, which owed him an hundred pence: and he laid hands on him, and took him by the throat, saying, Pay me that thou owest"* (Matthew 18:28). *The height of hypocrisy and unforgiveness,* we might think, yet this is exemplary of our due to God for His pardon of our immense sin debt—only in a much greater way—and our own lack of forgiveness toward others who owe us "pennies." There is not enough money in the whole world to ever pay the magnitude of our debt against our Creator, yet Christ fully freed us from it (Hebrews 9:15). How great is this undeserved love, as Ezra 9:13 proclaims, *"Seeing that thou our God hast punished us less than our iniquities deserve."* We could never bear what we truly deserve, for that is eternal damnation; praise the Lord that He shows us such great mercy. As a reflection of His grace, Christ commands us to forgive anyone who hurts, misuses, offends, or persecutes us: *"If any man have a quarrel against any: even as Christ forgave you, so also do ye"* (Colossians 3:13).

Is there any thing in your heart you are holding against someone who has hurt you? Even if you do not have a "grudge," what about that attitude of scorn you held toward another who worked ill against you—that bitterness toward someone who spoke hurtful words—or even that feeling of annoyance you felt toward a family member who wronged you? Isn't that a lack of mercy, grace, and forgiveness—a lack of *"always bearing about in the body the dying of the Lord Jesus, that the life also of Jesus might be made manifest in our body"* (II Corinthians 4:10)? Yes, this is a failure to forgive fellow neighbors who need our Savior's pardon just as much as we do. Oh, dear sister, evaluate your heart in the light of God's Word and weed out those areas in which the spirit of Christ does not flow through. *"If Christ be in you, the body is dead because of sin; but the Spirit is life because of righteousness"* (Romans 8:10).

Let us never forget our need for God's forgiveness and humbly ask for it to be shown toward us, as we live in gratefulness for the promise that His mercies *"are new every morning"* (Lamentations 3:23) through the blood of the Lamb. *"If Thou, LORD, shouldest mark iniquities, O Lord, who shall stand? But there is forgiveness with Thee, that Thou mayest be feared"* (Psalm 130:3-4)

"Lead us not into temptations, but deliver us from evil."

Knowing how weak we are in our flesh, and that our *"adversary the devil, as a roaring lion, walketh about, seeking whom he may devour"* (I Peter 5:8), we must beseech the Lord for His protection and strength. Our human nature is so sin-bent that there are few times when our focus flickers, by the power of God, to do righteousness. For this reason, we must ask for protection against temptations. Christ knows our frailty and the dust of our being and is willing to deliver; He asked the Father, *"I pray not that Thou shouldest take them out of the world, but that Thou shouldest keep them from the evil"* (John 17:15).

We must acknowledge our reliance on the Rock of our salvation, Who alone is victorious over every foe (Revelation 15:2). In Romans 15:30, Paul begged, *"I beseech you, brethren, for the Lord Jesus Christ's sake, and for the love of the Spirit, that ye strive together with me in your prayers to God for me."* He was asking for total exertion of the saint's prayers, as he realized he was engaged in a desperate unseen spiritual battle. We can bless those around us who face great spiritual and physical dangers by praying that temptation would not prevail in their hearts and that the Lord would protect them against what they are not able to bear, in accordance with the promise in I Corinthians 10:13, *"God is faithful, who will not suffer you to be tempted above that ye are able; but will with the temptation also make a way to escape, that ye may be able to bear it."* It is our privilege to be able to call upon the name of our Victor for deliverance on behalf of others: therefore, let us do so with boldness and faith.

prayers & answers

⁓I Kings 17:22-24

⁓II Kings 19:14-17

⁓I Chronicles 33:13

⁓II Chronicles 20

⁓Judges 16:28

⁓Ezra 8:22-23

⁓Job 6:23, 42:12

⁓Acts 7:59-60

⁓Acts 10

⁓Acts 16:26

Many beautiful prayers and answers are recorded in the Scriptures; studying the theme of prayer will bless you as you come to God's throne.

"For Thine is the kingdom,
and the power, and the glory, forever. Amen."

In this closing portion, Christ again glorifies the Father, acknowledging His dominion, power and worth. This exemplary prayer offers much wisdom and guidance to us as we spend time in our closets of prayer. Why don't you park a bookmark on this passage and study it more deeply each passing day, as you seek to develop a solid habit of life-transforming prayer?

standing in the gap

Daniel is a powerful example of devotion and faithfulness to the Lord in the Bible. At a very young age, he was exiled into a godless culture as a slave; however, rather than rejecting his righteous upbringing, we see his staunch trust in the one true God and commitment to godly convictions (Daniel 1:8). Though he was surrounded by pagan influences and persecution, *"Daniel purposed in his heart that he would not defile himself."* Those who hated Daniel knew that he had an irreproachable reputation; while plotting for a way to destroy him, they admitted, *"We shall not find any occasion against this Daniel, except we find it against him concerning the law of his God"* (Daniel 6:5). What a powerful example he is of holiness and obedience to the Lord!

I find Daniel's life-long habit of daily prayer, three times a day, to be especially inspiring. We see his ungodly king commanding the people to bow down to worship himself by threat of death, but are encouraged by Daniel's faithful refusal and trust in the Almighty: *"When Daniel knew that the writing was signed, he went into his house; and his windows being open in his chamber toward Jerusalem, he kneeled upon his knees three times a day, and prayed, and gave thanks before his God, as he did aforetime"* (Daniel 6:10). Notice that small phrase, "as he did aforetime"—Daniel had made prayer a well-established habit for the past eighty or more years of his life. What commitment! Imagine Daniel now as an aged man, making the effort to go into his private chamber three times each day, and kneeling on his knees as adoration for his God radiated from his countenance. This was a man in high authority who bore many responsibilities, but did not allow this to hinder his personal devotion to the Lord. Now, under the threat of death, his actions show that he would rather die and go to be with his Maker than obey the king's command to worship another god (Exodus 34:14). Through Daniel's commitment, the Lord miraculously delivered him from death in the lion's den, and also restored him to honor and authority. However, the ultimate result of Daniel's steadfastness is the exaltation of God's name throughout the entire land, for *"King Darius wrote unto all people...Every dominion of my kingdom men tremble and fear before the God of Daniel: for He is the living God, and stedfast for ever, and His kingdom that which shall not be destroyed, and His dominion shall be even unto the end"* (Daniel 6:25-26). This is the kind of unwavering commitment I desire to have for my Lord, for the praise of His righteous name—*Lord, make us worthy!*

biblical confession
～II Chronicles 30:22
～Ezra 9:6
～Nehemiah 1:7
～Daniel 9:5
～Psalms 32, 51

The recorded prayers of Daniel demonstrate his immense love for God. His prayer of praise to the Lord, Who revealed the king's dream for interpretation, is revealed in chapter two, when he praised, *"I thank Thee, and praise Thee, O Thou God of my fathers, who hast given me wisdom and might, and hast made known unto me now what we desired of Thee"* (Daniel 2:23). In chapter nine, we read of his ardent supplication, *"I set my face unto the Lord God,* to seek by prayer and supplications, with fasting, and sackcloth, and ashes" (verse 3), which demonstrates his personal burden for the Israelites' spiritual temperature. Immediately follows his notable prayer of confession and intercession on behalf of his exiled people: *"O Lord, hear; O Lord, forgive; O Lord, hearken and do; defer not, for Thine own sake, O my God: for Thy city and Thy people are called by Thy name"* (Daniel 9:19). Though he himself had honored and feared God, Daniel took upon himself the role of interceding for his people's vast sins: *"O Lord, to us belongeth confusion of face, to our kings, to our princes, and to our fathers, because we have sinned against Thee"* (verse 8). The Lord answered Daniel's humility in an awesome way—through the appearance of the angel Gabriel, who spoke words of affirmation and revelation (Daniel 9:21-22).

Daniel's example spurs me to greater faithfulness and responsibility in my prayer life—of interceding not only for those I know, but also for my people and my nation. We should take heed and humble ourselves before our God and King, fervently contending for the spiritual revival of the Church, remission of our sins, salvation of those who are lost, renewal of lives and hearts in our families, pastors, missionaries, and persecuted Christians around the world.

Intercession is a battle we all can wage on behalf of those in danger or need. Ask the Fountain of all good gifts to grant wisdom, guidance, spiritual light, and provision to His people (Ephesians 3:14-21). Isaiah contains many precious promises to claim for those who are walking through the shadow of persecution. For those who are in danger, embrace God's promise in Isaiah 43:2: *"When thou passest through the waters, I will be with thee; and through the rivers, they shall not overflow thee: when thou walkest through the fire, thou shalt not be burned; neither shall the flame kindle upon thee."* For those who are weary, ask the Lord to hold their hand, as Isaiah 42:6 says: *"I the LORD have called thee in righteousness, and will hold thine hand, and will keep thee, and give thee for a covenant of the people, for a light of the Gentiles."* In God alone rests the power to protect, forgive, and guide; let us boldly avail His throne, and thus witness His mighty provisions (Isaiah 25:9).

bold biblical prayer

God has given His people countless *"exceeding great and precious promises"* throughout His Word (II Peter 1:4). Bringing these Scriptures before the Lord encourages us to pray with Biblical confidence. I remember hearing a story about an elderly Christian gentleman who daily knelt in the loft of his old musty barn, where he kept a well-worn Bible, and earnestly contended for the faith. One night a preacher accompanied this godly man to pray, and was awed to hear him begin with utmost boldness and fearless confidence, pointing to God's promises throughout the Scriptures, recalling His past faithfulness, and asking in faith for Biblical provision. How enriched our prayers would be if we knew the promises and prayers given in God's Word, and brought them to heaven's doorstep in faith! Our Father is willing and eager to bestow upon us spiritual wisdom, enlightenment, protection, and deeper Christ-like

spiritual prayers
- Numbers 6:24-27
- Colossians 1:9-12
- I Corinthians 16:24
- II Corinthians 13:11,14
- II Thessalonians 1:11-12
- II Thessalonians 2:15-17
- II Thessalonians 3:3-5
- Hebrews 13:20-21
- Philippians 1:9-11
- Ephesians 1:15-19
- Ephesians 3:14-21
- I Peter 5:10

love, if we will but ask. Matthew 7:7 promises, *"Ask, and it shall be given you; seek, and ye shall find; knock, and it shall be opened unto you."* Thoughtlessly praying, *Lord, please bless ___ and ___ today,* neglects the many specific spiritual needs we have before the Lord and fails to claim the precious promises He has for every believer.

I have sought to memorize Biblical prayers, so that as I pray for others, my words can be formed after His own. For example, Paul's prayer for the Ephesians in 3:14-21 is a beautiful pattern of intercession: *Father of the Lord Jesus, I ask that You would grant my family, according to Your glorious riches, to be strengthened with might, by Christ's Spirit in the inner man, that Christ may richly dwell in our hearts by faith today, and that You would root and ground us in Your love so that we can know with all saints what is its breadth, and length, and depth, and height, and to know that glorious love which passeth knowledge, that we may be filled with Your fullness, for Your glory...*

> Though, in the early stages [of prayer]...all the time seems spent in bringing the mind back from its wanderings and fixing it again on prayer, they are not moments lost. Such *discipline* will exercise the muscles of the will, and the day will dawn when the sweetest *meditation*...will be possible even amid distraction.
>
> (WILLIAM SANGSTER)

Bring to the throne of mercy God's beautiful promises in faith—and be richly blessed! This is my prayer for you: *"The God of all grace, who hath called us unto his eternal glory by Christ Jesus, after that ye have suffered a while, make you perfect, stablish, strengthen, settle you"* (I Peter 5:10).

alone with God

Realizing the glorious gift that prayer is, what a great folly it would be for us—as redeemed children of the One who secured its privilege—to neglect it. I encourage you to commit yourself to a goal of daily prayer, in devotion to the Lord and obedience to His command, *"pray without ceasing"* (I Thessalonians 5:17). Set a reachable amount of time to pray each day; even just ten minutes of prayer every morning will reap more fruit than you can ever imagine. This discipline is the solid key through which great victories will be won for the glory of Christ, and is a habit which will revolutionize your life—as well as those around you and untold future generations. James 5:16 is a great encouragement, *"The effectual fervent prayer of a righteous man availeth much."* Susanna Wesley was a woman of daily, eternally-minded prayer; one can only imagine how much impact this had on the spiritual depth of her nineteen children, especially in the effectiveness of her sons' widespread proclamation of the Gospel—and revival around the world.

Establishing a daily prayer time with the Lord will require commitment; hindrances *will* arise, but they must be overcome, not allowed to take away our focus—just as Daniel did not let death threats to hinder him. We all can make excuses about not having time to pray, but that simply is not true: our Creator has given every human twenty-four hours in every day, and we fill every one of those 1,440 minutes with some kind of activity. Many of us spend more time "living life" and eating than with the Lord. Yet, when Christ is our Redeemer and the most important Person in this entire universe, how can we say we have "no time to pray"? When Jesus is our only source of power and grace, how can we *not* come to Him on our knees? Without the strength He bestows through prayer, we are utterly hopeless.

What about waking during those long, quiet hours of the night for uninterrupted prayer? Or rising in the wee morning hours, as we see of David (Psalm 5:3) and of the Prince of prayer (Mark 1:35)? I know a dear mother of many children who awakens every night for an hour of prayer. Although her body must be weary

after the day's responsibilities, she is not willing that her time with Jesus should flee—the victories won in prayer simply are not worth forfeiting. True men and women of God who spend hours each day at the throne of Christ, will lead the lives of spiritual victory, for they hide themselves in the only Source of power. We *can*—simply must—make time to pray.

Confining our flesh to the discipline of prayer requires toil and faithfulness, yet its establishment must be top priority.

∾ Go to a quiet place where you will be uninterrupted, and find a position that helps you wholly focus on prayer—whether that be on your knees, pacing the floor, or praying aloud. *"I cried with my whole heart"* (Psalm 119:145).

∾ Open your Bible and prayer journal. Bring Biblical prayers and praises to the Lord as you recall His faithful provisions; recall promises and commands from the Scriptures in prayer, exalting the name of God the Father and Christ the Son (II Thessalonians 1:12). *"The word of the Lord endureth for ever. And this is the word which by the gospel is preached unto you"* (I Peter 1:25). Follow the standard of Christ's exemplary prayer in Matthew chapter six.

∾ Discipline your mind to stay focused; this will be difficult, but is a battle which must be waged, not avoided. As time goes on, your mind will become more self-controlled (James 4:7). *"Commit thy works unto the LORD, and thy thoughts shall be established"* (Proverbs 16:3). Consider having a piece of paper handy for anything that comes to mind that needs to be attended to later, so that you can write it down immediately and continue in prayer.

~ Pray specifically (Romans 15:30) in the will of God (Matthew 26:42, Hebrews 10:9).

~ Entreat Christ for victory in your life, relying on Him for all spiritual growth (II Corinthians 10:17, 12:9). Ask for more focus and love for Him, because you cannot do anything good alone (Psalm 18:1, 116:1, 119:47, 119:159).

> *Prayer should be like an open phone line between us and our Lord. Throughout the day, communion with Him must continue as we ask Christ for His direction, and then listen for His leading.*
>
> I THESSALONIANS 5:17

~ Worship the Lord in the beauty of His holiness (I Chronicles 16:29) and praise Him for His provisions (Psalm 9:1).

May our Lord and Savior Jesus Christ grant blessing as you develop a solid habit of prayer, so that when you fall to your knees, the halls of Heaven ring with joy—for Christ delights in our bold intercession and reliance on Him, and joys to answer our prayers.

heritage of God's faithfulness

Recording prayer requests and God's perfect answers is a faith-deepening experience, as it shows His incessant[4] faithfulness at work. *"I will sing of the mercies of the LORD for ever: with my mouth will I make known Thy faithfulness to all generations"* (Psalm 89:1). There are many ways to record God's provision in our lives; I currently use a prayer notebook which has designated tabs for praises, requests, thanksgivings, and answers to prayer. I also write prayer requests on my calendar and each morning am reminded who to keep in prayer that day. In a notebook, you can make the columns "Request Date," "Prayer Request," "Date answered," and "Answer." You can also use a spiral 3x5-inch card holder with different prayer categories ("Family," "Seeking God's Will," "Ministries," "Church," "Country," "Friends," "Missionaries"). I encourage you to find a method that is effective for you, for through keeping a prayer journal, God's faithfulness will be preserved. This will encourage you to recall His wondrous provisions throughout your life. Future generations will also have the faith-building privilege of looking back and witnessing His goodness (Psalm 103:2). God encourages His people to record His works for this very reason—that His perpetual trustworthiness would be passed on for others to trust and fear (Psalm 40:3). In I Samuel 7:12, Samuel set up a stone of remembrance and *"called the name of it Eben-*

> *thanksgiving*
>
> " Daily, praise the Lord for His benefits. Psalms 119:164 inspired me to daily write down seven thanksgivings; this has been an effective exercise in turning my mind to constant praise. "

---

[4] INCESSANT. *Unceasing; unintermitted.*

ezer, saying, Hitherto hath the LORD helped us," as a testimony to future progeny. Psalm seventy-eight says, *"I will open my mouth in a parable...which we have heard and known, and our fathers have told us. We will not hide them from their children, shewing to the generation to come the praises of the LORD, and His strength, and His wonderful works that He hath done"* (Psalm 78:2-4). Let us diligently delight in keeping "ebenezers" in our own lives, *"written for the generation to come: and the people which shall be created shall praise the LORD"* (Psalm 102:18).

Following are a few personal illustrations of God's provisions I have been overjoyed to witness in the span of a few months; may the Lord Jesus, our Jehovah-Jireh, be glorified!

 A young wife and mother we know was on the brink of death, with little predicted hope of recovery; many believers constantly interceded on behalf of her life and family. Within a few weeks, she was miraculously healed and is now able to care for her family once again.

 The Lord has continually answered intercession and fasting on behalf of the Smith family, who is seeking to serve Christ despite extreme opposition and difficult circumstances. The Lord is faithful to protect His people!

 We prayed for Jane's healing from cancer as well as for her salvation. Several months later, her cancer miraculously disappeared; we continue to pray for her redemption.

 Our family has prayed for the spiritual encouragement of a father we know, and God has amazingly answered by working in his heart and turning him to see and fill the needs of his family.

"I will praise Thy name; for Thou hast done wonderful things; Thy counsels of old are faithfulness and truth" (Isaiah 25:1). These

joyous answers to prayer are not "extraordinary" examples—they are simply illustrations of God's faithfulness to hear and answer our prayers, for He delights in those who will *"call unto Me"* (Jeremiah 33:3). We should delight in daily recording His perfect answers to our needs and entreaties, that we may praise His name for His inerrant provision. Keeping a prayer journal has been a tremendous joy for me, and will continue to be an encouragement to look back upon and praise the name of my Provider.

All prayers are not answered immediately; some requests will remain petitions throughout an entire lifetime. However, the Lord desires our unceasing diligence in prayer, especially those requests which are clearly in accordance with His revealed will in the Scriptures. We must never cease from faithful prayer even if the answer seems long in coming, for when we give up, we demonstrate shameful doubt in the Jehovah-Jireh Who *delights* in giving good gifts to His people (Isaiah 42:1). The fact that the Creator of the universe is waiting to give His people good and precious gifts (Jeremiah 32:41-42) causes my heart to bow in wonder. Therefore, it is our privilege and responsibility to faithfully knock on Heaven's gates, praying until our prayers are answered or until the Lord reveals that it is not His will to grant our request. This kind of boldness and perseverance at the throne of mercy would be preposterous[5] if we were not invited there, but our Lord has *commanded* us to pray without ceasing (I Thessalonians 5:17)!

In Luke eighteen, we find a beautiful example of a poor widow who persistently approached a wicked and merciless judge, pleading for justice to be done toward one who had wronged her. Although he feared not God nor cared for any man, the judge finally relented, tired by her persistence—and

---

[5] PREPOSTEROUS. *Absurd; contrary to nature or reason.*

performed justice on her behalf. Verse seven points out, *"Shall not God avenge His own elect, which cry day and night unto Him, though He bear long with them?"* Jesus commands His people through this parable, *"Men ought always to pray, and not to faint"* (Luke 18:1), for shall not a God Who loves us, delight in answering our prayers and in bestowing mercy to us?

on the altar

Vigilant[6] prayer sanctifies the life of a believer, for it is one of God's means of aligning our hearts with His will. It also prepares us to receive His will and to glorify His name for His impeccable answer. In the garden of Gethsemane, we find Christ wrestling in prayer, so much that He was sweating blood—and then coming to that point of unreserved submission, saying, *"Not as I will, but as Thou wilt"* (Matthew 26:39), even when it meant drinking the cup of God's wrath (Revelation 16:19). As we wrestle in prayer, we must come to that climax when we simply leave the request there at the feet of our Father, submitting as Christ did, *"Not as I will, but as Thou wilt."* When we are brought into alignment with God's will, we can trust Him for the truly best answer, knowing that He has an infinite plan for our good (Jeremiah 29:11), and that we are ultimately dependant on His sovereign provision.

Romans 8:28 assures us, *"We know that all things work together for good to them that love God, to them who are the called according to His purpose."* God has a plan for His people, and answers their prayers in His own perfect time and way—He is never late, never slack. *"How precious also are Thy thoughts unto me, O God! how great is the sum of them!"* (Psalm 139:17) He has the divine wisdom to answer our petitions whenever and however He sees fit.

---

[6] VIGILANT. *Watchful; circumspect; attentive to discover or avoid danger.*

While waiting for God's answer to our prayers, we are called to continue in faithful prayer and trust Him for the out-come—to surrender our lives to His incredible goodness, believing that no matter what God's timing is, or how He answers, that He is unquestionably *good*. The Psalmist in 130:5 says that *"I wait for the LORD, my soul doth wait, and in His word do I hope,"* and hoping in God's Word is exactly how we must wait. Psalm 37:4,7 offers beautiful advice for the waiting: *"Trust in the LORD, and do good... Rest in the LORD, and wait patiently for Him."* Filling our minds with His precious promises is a beautiful way to quiet our impatient hearts while anticipating God's answer, for He has *"given unto us exceeding great and precious promises: that by these ye might be partakers of the divine nature"* (II Peter 1:4).

promises
TO THE WAITING
~Psalm 25:3, 5
~Psalm 25:21
~Psalm 27:14
~Psalm 37:34
~Psalm 40:1
~Psalm 52:9
~Psalm 59:9
~Psalm 62:5
~Psalm 123:2
~Isaiah 25:9
~Isaiah 33:2
~Isaiah 49:23
~Isaiah 64:4
~Micah 7:7

There have been seasons in my spiritual walk when a desire or need has been laid on my heart strongly, and although these issues have been matters of fervent intercession, the Lord has sometimes answered, "wait." While waiting, at times the fear has crept in my heart—*maybe the Lord is slow to hear my supplications?* We may encounter situations when doubt enters our mind and our trust begins to wane—however, girded with the shied of faith (Ephesians 6:16) and reminded of God's promises, we are to reflect on His proven faithfulness, and shatter every doubt in Christ's sublime wisdom. These seasons are used by the Lord to increase our faith in His sovereignty (Hebrews 11:1).

How can we ever question God's plan and timing, when His view is eternal, and ours limited; when His thoughts are so vast, and we are finite? *"For as the Heavens are higher than the earth, so are My ways higher than your ways, and My thoughts than your thoughts"* (Isaiah 55:9). Picture a young child asking his wise and loving father for a certain toy. Maybe the father replies, "Wait, my dear child," for he has a far greater gift in mind. How foolish would it be for the child to impatiently fret and complain because his father has said he must wait? Wouldn't the young child do well to sit patiently and trust, with a child-like expectant faith, in his wise father who truly cares more deeply than can be imagined? Our heavenly Father loves us so much more than we can ever fathom, and He delights in giving us good and gracious gifts—*"exceeding abundantly above all that we ask or think"* (Ephesians 3:20)! *"Many, O LORD my God, are Thy wonderful works which Thou hast done, and Thy thoughts which are to us-ward: they cannot be reckoned up in order unto Thee"* (Psalm 40:5). In a much greater way than any loving earthly father, our Lord delights in listening to His children's requests and in granting those desires for our own good—and much more besides! Therefore, we must trust our Abba, our dear Father, and His unchanging promises, for *"this is the confidence that we have in Him, that, if we ask any thing according to His will, He heareth us"* (I John 5:14). What an awesome and gracious heavenly Father we have!

In Revelation, we find that we not only trust the Lord because His plan is irreproachable, but also because He is unutterably worthy: *"Thou art worthy, O Lord, to receive glory and honour and power: for Thou hast created all things, and for Thy pleasure they are and were created"* (Revelation 4:11). God is worthy—infinitely worthy of everything—*and more.* Can that truth ever be proclaimed enough? Our Father is clothed in majesty, wisdom, justice, holi-

ness, love, mercy—He is just over-
whelmingly *worthy*! This fact alone
gives us reason to trust Him forever, no matter what He brings into
our path, for He deserves our trust.
*"We do not present our supplications
before Thee for our righteousnesses, but
for Thy great mercies"* (Daniel 9:18).
Everything we have is a gift of His
grace—every breath of fresh air, ev-

> " Every second that
> God delays judg-
> ment on the world
> is simply a second of
> grace and mercy that
> we do not *deserve*. "
> (STEPHEN BRATTON)

ery cloud in the sky, every blade of grass, every minute wherein
He stokes the fires of the sun, every nerve through which we
feel, every drink of clear water, every earthly joy, every physical
comfort—and then every innumerable promise of His unfailing, unmerited love—God is the Author of every blessing, not
one of which we deserve (read Psalm104). As Daniel 9:9 says,
*"To the Lord our God belong mercies and forgivenesses, though we have
rebelled against Him."* God's goodness toward us (Psalm 40:5) is
unmitigated; therefore, may our commitment to trust Him, as a
matter of choice, be as unmovable as Job's, who said—*"Though
He slay me, yet will I trust in Him"* (Job 13:15). Amen! *"Blessed
be the God and Father of our Lord Jesus Christ, which according to
His abundant mercy hath begotten us again unto a lively hope by the
resurrection of Jesus Christ"* (I Peter 1:3). Let us trust our heavenly
Father for His perfect timing and provision, for *"no good thing
will He withhold from them that walk uprightly"* (Psalm 84:11).

at heaven's doorstep

If we as God's people take seriously this weighty calling of
prayer, boldly claiming His promises—how will our lives, families, future generations, churches, and entire world be changed

for the exaltation of our Lord and the furtherance of His Kingdom? We will never know unless we do it. Let us fall on our knees, knowing that we have no other hope outside of our God's power. Let us hide ourselves in the watches of the night, crying out for Him to *"send forth labourers into His harvest"* (Luke 10:2)—for the days of our Bridegroom's return draw nigh (I Thessalonians 5:2), yet the harvest remains great.

Christ asked in Luke 18:8 the sad question, *"When the Son of man cometh, shall He find faith on the earth?"* May our Savior find us with faith, storming Heaven's doorstep day after day—reaping an eternal harvest through the power of prayer. He has purchased prayer's priceless privilege—and alone brings the victory. *"Seeing then that we have a great high priest, that is passed into the heavens, Jesus the Son of God, let us hold fast our profession. Let us therefore come boldly unto the throne of grace, that we may obtain mercy, and find grace to help in time of need"* (Hebrews 4:14,16).

"Let us be much employed in the duty of prayer; let us pray with all prayer and supplication; let us live prayerful lives, continuing instant in prayer, watching thereunto with all perseverance; praying always without ceasing, earnestly, and not fainting."

jonathan edwards

"O *Christ*, He is the fountain,

the deep, sweet *well* of love!

The *streams* of earth I've tasted

more deep I'll drink above:

There to an *ocean* fullness

His mercy doth expand,

and glory, *glory* dwelleth

in Emmanuel's land."

anne cousin

all these . *vain things*

THE LEAVES of her well-worn Bible blew gently in the breeze, as the young girl gazed at the gushing water before her. The words of Psalm forty-two, her current Scripture memory passage, rolled through her mind. *"As the hart panteth after the water brooks, so panteth my soul after Thee, O God. My soul thirsteth for God, for the living God: when shall I come and appear before God?"* She meditated on these magnificent words; day after day, she had been studying them, and her heart was deeply touched by the vivid picture the Psalmist had painted of a parched deer. *Father, I desire truly that my heart would yearn after You alone,* she quietly prayed. *The things of this world often distract my focus, to my dismay; You alone are worthy and are all that my soul can thrive upon!* Her musings were abruptly broken when she noticed a parting in the wooded brush across the creek before her—and a beautiful deer stepped into the clearing and headed toward the waterbrook. Holding her breath with excitement, the damsel's heart swelled with joy as she watched the deer intake the clear water with satisfaction. She whispered to her Maker, *Thank you,*

Lord Jesus, for this beautiful demonstration of how thirsty I must be for your Water—the Scriptures! Just like this deer relies daily on the life-giving sustenance of this fresh water, so my heart is fed by Your own love and breath each day through your Word. The maiden recalled something her brother had mentioned before about thirsty deer—a deer will not notice you approach it until you are very close: its focus and need for water is so intent that it will not be moved. A chord was struck in her heart as she realized that her own thirst for the living water of God must be unwavering and undistracted by all else. *Father, thank You for this rich analogy! Please satisfy my heart alone with Your Word, as with a bubbling brook of joy in the knowledge of Your truth; may nothing of this world spoil Your fulfillment of my soul.*

∾

*H*ow impassioned is your heart for the Lord Jesus and for His Word? Is your thirst for Him so unquenchable that your soul refuses the lure of temporal trinkets (Psalm 63:1)? Does Christ alone hold your focus and kindle your life's ardor? Can you say, *"My soul longeth, yea, even fainteth for the courts of the LORD: my heart and my flesh crieth out for the living God"* (Psalm 84:2)? Is your meditation of Him sweet (Psalm 104:34)?

"The whole world lieth in wickedness" (I John 5:19) and presents countless hindrances which can steal our focus and love for Jesus Christ. The carnal, fleshly "fast food" of this world must not be suffered to take our minds from the satisfying, pure delights of God, for Colossians 3:2 commands, *"Set your affection on things above, not on things on the earth."* Our hearts must stand unmoved by all other trite affections and set upon the One Who alone is worthy of *all* of our affections (Deuteronomy 10:12).

apple of my eye

The "apple of the eye" is the most valuable portion of the eye—the pupil. When you get very close to someone, you can see your own reflection there. Those who desire a close relationship with the Lord, so close that they can look right into His face and see the "apple of His eye," are the ones Psalm 24:5 says will receive His blessing—righteousness from the God of our salvation. This preeminent, close relationship with Christ should be our greatest goal (Psalm 24:6).

Is Christ at the "apple of your eye"? Are you standing so close to Him that nothing of this world attracts your glance? As we seek the Lord, our great desire should be to rid our lives of anything that is in the way of a close communion, vision, and knowledge of the One Who alone matters—*"For what is your life? It is even a vapour, that appeareth for a little time, and then vanisheth away"* (James 4:14). Jesus must ever increase (John 3:30) in our hearts as our strongest and only love—more precious to us than all the world. The life of Sarah Edwards is a beautiful example of one filled to the brim with God's love and ever-expanding grace, because she spent her life gazing into His face. She delighted to live in the presence of her Savior, and that communion worked her own sanctification and then was reflected to her husband, children, and others (II Corinthians 4:6). She once wrote of her spiritual awakening in Christ, "I was entirely swallowed up in God, as my only portion, and His honor and glory was the object of my supreme desire and delight... At the same time, my heart and soul all flowed out in love to Christ, so that there seemed to be a constant flowing and reflowing of heavenly and diving love from Christ's heart to mine." The close communion with the Lord that Sarah experienced can be ours if we will set our eyes only to Him: *"Look unto me, and be ye saved, all the ends of* the earth: *for I am God, and there is none else*" (Isaiah 45:22).

As we look and cling to our Prince, allowing no distractions or hindering affections to take root in our hearts, the fleeting idols of this world will dim to our Heaven-focused hearts. Seeking our Lord and being captivated by Him is worth losing everything of this ephemeral[1] world to gain only one thing; the apostle Paul said, "*I count all things but loss for the excellency of the knowledge of Christ Jesus my Lord: for Whom I have suffered the loss of all things, and do count them but dung*"—why was he willing to lose all of these things?—"*that I may win Christ, and be found in Him*" (Philippians 3:8-9). Truly Christ alone is worth everything! What significance do the fleeting issues of life have to the eyes which have His eternal glories in focus? All that matters is that which will be revealed by fire on that final day before His throne. Let fleshly and worldly idols, trends, and fads pass by. They cannot waver a heart that prays, "Lord, in place of all the joys of the world grant me the sweet anointing of your Spirit, and instead of the loves of this life, pour in the love of Your name" (Thomas á Kempis).

fast for feasting

It has been important for me to frequently examine my heart, especially in the busy seasons of life, to make sure that Christ is truly "the apple of my eye"—at the forefront of my desires, thoughts, purposes, and actions. Closely monitoring my heart has been vital for my spiritual ardency and revival, for so easily evanescent[2] "idols"[3] creep in and cloud my spiritual desire and love for God. How prone to wander is this human heart! Refocusing on that most vital part of my day—sitting at the feet of

---

[1] EPHEMERAL. *Short-lived; existing or continuing for a short time only.*

[2] EVANESCENT. *Vanishing; liable to dissipation, like vapor.*

[3] IDOL. *Any thing on which we set our affections; that to which we indulge an excessive and sinful attachment.*

my Master in the Word—helps me to keep an eternal focus on what truly matters in this short breath of life. I must frequently ask the Lord to "awaken" my heart with zeal for Him and to give me more grace to love Him more, echoing Psalm 119:88, *"Quicken me after Thy lovingkindness; so shall I keep the testimony of Thy mouth."*

Evaluating every realm in our life is vital—friendships, social interactions, music, hobbies, clothing, pictures, books, internet, social media, current styles, reputation or recognition, and even financial status, posses-sions, and self-image. *"He is before all things"* (Colossians 1:17). All of our duties and responsibilities in life must fall under His headship in our hearts, and if something is distracting our love for our Savior, it must be relinquished.

> As we behold His *glorious* face, all those *vain* things which charm us most *vanish* into dust.

Redefining my concentration on Christ and His Word through different disciplines has been very beneficial for the sharpening of my spiritual focus. One summer I decided to "diet" from all books except the Scriptures, to revive my zeal and anticipation for God's Word. I quickly realized that books heav-ily influence my thought-life, and I was blessed by the time to focus solely on the only Book which shall stand forever (Isaiah 40:8). Christ must be as sweet as honey to our spiritual taste, for He alone can feed our souls (Psalm 119:103). Stories or light books can tend to eat away our relish for His Word, and can also induce an attitude of discontentment, which saps an earnest ex-pectation for the Bible's soul-nourishment. It is important that we use discretion in what we allow to go into our minds; there are so many books and activities that can leave us with unrealistic emotions, expectations, and thoughts which take away a love for God's truth and for pure beauty. Let us wisely select what we read and listen to and reject all that is not God-honoring, in accordance with Philippians 4:8, *"Finally, brethren, whatsoever things are true, whatsoever things are honest, whatsoever things are just, whatsoever things are pure, whatsoever things are lovely, whatsoever things are of good report; if there be any virtue, and if there be any praise, think on these things."*

> See that your *relish* for the Bible be above every other enjoyment, and the moment you begin to feel greater relish for any other book, lay it down till you have sought deliverance from such a snare, and obtained from the Holy Spirit an intenser relish, a keener appetite for the *word of God.*
>
> (HORATIUS BONAR)

I also have undertaken media and internet "fasts," which have helped refocus my concentration on the Rock of my salvation. With the constant flow of needless, albeit interesting, trivia that media provides, I have learned that I must make a choice to stay my mind on Christ, for *"Thou wilt keep him in perfect peace, whose mind is stayed on Thee"* (Isaiah 26:3). When we eliminate the vain trifles that surround us from our mind, and choose to rest our thoughts on that all-sufficient Cross, His peace and love will gracefully sustain us.

Abstaining from certain foods we enjoy, or fasting completely from food, can also be a means of seeking the face of the Lord and approaching Him with an earnest, yet humble, desire to know Him more intimately. Disciplining our bodies in this way—hungering for our Maker as for our own bodily nourishment—is a beautiful and needful reminder of the One Who nourishes our soul as food supports our body. Jesus alone is our all-providing Bread of life, as John 6:51 says, *"I am the living bread which came down from heaven: if any man eat of this bread, he shall live for ever: and the bread that I will give is My flesh, which I will give for the life of the world."* Jesus Christ truly *"satisfieth the longing soul, and filleth the hungry soul with goodness"* (Psalm 107:9).

There are so many other temporal areas that can hinder our spiritual reliance on God, and can be refrained from in order to yoke our desires under the lordship of Jesus Christ. Each of us must honestly evaluate our heart before the Lord, in light of His Word, and strip ourselves of anything that weakens our love for Him. Through discipline, we can strive to avoid the mastery of carnal desires and thoughts, *"casting down imaginations, and every high thing that exalteth itself against the knowledge of God, and bringing into captivity every thought to the obedience of Christ"* (II Corinthians 10:5)—harnessing everything under subjection and obedience to our Master Jesus Christ. We must apply self-discipline and make the necessary sacrifices to place the Lord our God first in our heart, soul, and mind. He loves a contrite, wholly yielded heart (Psalm 34:18, 51:17).

In Matthew 6:16, our Lord Jesus taught purity of motive in all fasting: *"Moreover when ye fast, be not, as the hypocrites, of a sad countenance: for they disfigure their faces, that they may appear unto men to fast. Verily I say unto you, they have their reward."* As we seek the face of the Lord, we must do so in humility and privacy. I encourage you to study God's mind on the topic of fasting, whether it is from food or another area of life, in Isaiah chapter fifty-eight. What was the condition of the people at this time (verses 1-2)? Did God accept their fasts (verses 3-5)? What is a true fast to the Lord (verses 6-7)? What is the outcome of a true God-honoring fast that is rewarded (verses 8-12)? The Lord offers incredible blessings to those who truly yearn to know and honor His glorious name.

manna from heaven

Our Father assuredly *"is a rewarder of them that diligently seek Him"* (Hebrews 11:6)—and how worth seeking and knowing He is! He honors the heart which approaches Him with an avid desire to be filled with the One Who satisfies our longing souls (John 6:51). Oh dear friend, I so long that you would experience His rich goodness for yourself and truly be filled with the Bread of Life, the Living Water (John 4:10), and the Honey out of the Rock (Psalm 81:16)! Whatever you must do to place Jesus first in your life—that is such a minute sacrifice in light of His eternal blessings and goodness. Make Christ the apple of your eye! Stay your mind upon Him and feed upon His beauties? What is that area for you, that can be laid aside for a length of time, as you seek your Master? Is something of this vain world distracting your spiritual ardor? Come to the Lord with a humble attitude, beseeching His grace to teach you as you earnestly seek His

biblical fasts

- Jesus Christ (Matthew 4:2)
- David (II Samuel 12:16)
- Nehemiah (Nehemiah 1:4)
- Esther (Esther 4:16)
- Ezra (Ezra 8:23)
- Daniel (Daniel 9:3)
- Anna (Luke 2:37)
- Cornelius (Acts 10:30)
- the Apostles (Acts 13:3)

Study the motivation, approach, and answers to these fasts

face (I Chronicles 16:11), and ask Him to circumcise your heart, *"to love the LORD thy God with all thine heart, and with all thy soul"* (Deuteronomy 30:6). As you rejoice in Jesus and delight in His

Word, you will find that He is more fulfilling to your soul than every earthly joy combined. Make Him alone the apple of your eye; pour all of your energy and life into knowing Him, and the ocean of His love and grace will engulf you (Psalm 86:10).

Only when we are basking in the truths of God's righteousness and placing Him first in our vision—only then, will the treasures of Heaven steadily grow dazzling to our wondering eyes. Psalm 17:15 gives the restful sigh of the one who abides in Christ, beholding His face: *"As for me, I will behold Thy face in righteousness: I shall be satisfied, when I awake, with Thy likeness."* All those vain trinkets that charm us most—assuredly dim in the light of Jesus' glory and grace!

"Father, I want to know Thee, but my cowardly heart fears to give up its toys...Please root from my heart all those things which I have cherished so long and which have become a very part of my living self, so that Thou mayest enter and dwell there without a rival. Then shalt Thou make the place of Thy feet glorious. Then shall my heart have no need of the sun to shine in it, for Thyself wilt be the light of it, and there shall be no night there. In Jesus' name. Amen."

a . w .   t o z e r

"O LORD, in the

simplicity of my heart

I offer myself unto Thee this day,

in humble submission, for a

sacrifice of perpetual praise,

and to be Thy servant forever."

∾

thomas à kempis

5

a *living* sacrifice

*T*HE CHIEF END of man—the very purpose for which he was created by God—is to glorify the Lord his Maker, *"For of Him, and through Him, and to Him, are all things"* (Romans 11:36). Isaiah 43:7 says, *"Every one that is called by My name: for I have created Him for My glory, I have formed him; yea, I have made him."* We owe to God everything, for we only exist by His power and mercy; *"In Him we live, and move, and have our being"* (Acts 17:28). How do we glorify our Creator? In I Chronicles 16:29, we read, *"Give unto the LORD the glory due unto His name: bring an offering, and come before Him: worship the LORD in the beauty of holiness."* We glorify the Lord by bringing the glory due to His worthy name and exalting Him before others (Psalm 29:2). Glorifying God consists of our worship—a demonstration of our adoration of and praise of Him (Psalm 50:23).

The Lord God must be the center of our worship, because He is the only One worthy of it. He is holy (Leviticus 11:44), He is righteous (Psalm 116:5, Hebrews 1:9), He is the faithful witness (Revelation 1:5), He is eternal (Revelation 1:4,8,11,17)—the beginning and the end: "*I am Alpha and Omega, the beginning and the ending, saith the Lord, which is, and which was, and which is to come, the Almighty*" (Revelation 1:8). Who can fully grasp the greatness of God's splendor and infinity, when we as humans can only see a small quantum[1] of its expanse? What depths of worship His glorious nature demands!

God's untold character presents substantial reason for us to bow in worship of Him throughout eternity—however, there is yet another colossal[2] motivation for our adoration. As Revelation 1:5 revels, "*Unto Him that loved us, and washed us from our sins in His own blood, and hath made us kings and priests unto God and His Father; to Him be glory and dominion for ever and ever.*" The omnipotent

worship God for His...
Immutability (Malachi 3:6)
Glorious names (Nehemiah 9:5)
Power (Psalm 62:11)
Sovereign plan (Romans 8:28)
Love (John 17:23)
Mercy (Psalm 57:10, 86:15)
Salvation (Psalm 118:21)

Root of Jesse (Isaiah 11:10) has shown unlimited love toward us in the redemption of our souls, at the price of His own blood; this compels us to worship Him with *all* of our being. Christ Jesus has *loved* us and made us kings and priests unto God! All glory and laud be to Him forever and ever (Romans 15:11)! We owe all worship and adoration to Him for this unspeakable mercy manifested on our behalf. And this is the purpose for which we were redeemed by the Lamb of God.

[1] QUANTUM. *The quantity; the amount.*

[2] COLOSSAL. *Very large; huge; gigantic.*

sacrifice of worship

If the very reason we were saved by Christ is to worship Him, shouldn't we know how to do it for His pleasure? When I originally thought of the term "worship," a currently-promoted concept of music, praise, and fleshly arousal came to mind. However, the Scriptures must be our guide; we are told that *"they that worship Him must worship Him in spirit and in truth"* (John 4:24)—and we know that truth (Psalm 119:142) is found alone in God's Word (John 5:39). As I began studying the Lord's thoughts on this topic, I discovered that He has laid out a beautiful and life-transforming pattern of worship in the Scriptures.

"Worship" means "to adore, to pay divine honor to, or to reverence with supreme respect and veneration." The first appearance of the term "worship" in the Scriptures is very enlightening to how we can worship God in a prescribed manner. Genesis 22:5 relates, *"Abraham said unto his young men, abide ye here with the ass; and I and the lad will go yonder and worship, and come again to you."* Abraham's purpose in ascending the mountain was to worship his God, and he took along the free-will offering which the Lord had asked of him (Genesis 22:2): Isaac, his well-loved, only son. In this act of obedience, Abraham demonstrated unimaginable faith, for God had promised that from his seed would be made a great nation. Abraham believed that God could work something great even out of this seemingly impossible situation—even if he sacrificed his son in obedience to God's command. In Hebrews 11:9 we find that he trusted the Lord to raise Isaac from the dead. In this aspect of Abraham's worship, we learn that our free-will sacrifice of obedience to God must be offered in complete faith, even when that route may lead through the dark shadow of the death of our will. The result of this sacrificial worship is a walk of obedience to God, as we take one step at a time in accordance with God's revealed will in the Scriptures, trusting Him to fulfill His promises. We see from Abraham's example—as well as Isaac's submission in laying himself on the altar—that worship involves complete surrender of our will.

Abraham "went all the way" in obedience to the Lord. He was fully surrendered, for he moved to initiate this sorrow-filled sacrifice. However, the Lord saw Abraham's heart of submission and called down from heaven, *"Lay not thine hand upon the lad, neither do thou any thing unto him: for now I know that thou fearest God, seeing thou hast not withheld thy son, thine only son from Me"* (Genesis 22:12). Abraham had demonstrated true worship to the Lord, in the act of willingly laying down his dearest possession on the altar, and therefore, the Lord blessed him—for Abraham looked up and saw a ram caught in the thicket (Genesis 22:13). Who can imagine the depths of gratitude felt in his heart at that moment! One's life of worship will be filled with overwhelming thankfulness for God's provision for our sacrifice of worship—solely through the ultimate Sacrifice which was provided to take away our sins (I John 2:2); the Lamb of God Who was slain on a tree (Romans 3:25).

> *worship* is the complete self-sacrifice of all that I love that would keep me from receiving the Lord's *provision.*
> (DONNA MORGAN)

As we see from Abraham's sacrifice[3] in Genesis 22, worship is more than an organized weekly time of "worship music." Our true sacrifice of worship includes a life walked worthy of the Lord (Romans 12-16), trusting in His immovable promises,

---

[3] SACRIFICE. *To offer to God in homage or worship, by killing...on the altar...as an atonement.*

obeying Him in faith, and then living in the joy which results from our worship.

an offering well-pleasing

So what is our sacrifice of worship today, as New Testament believers? In the Old Testament, Jehovah's people worshipped Him through sacrificing the prescribed free-will offerings on the altar (Leviticus 1:3). On Calvary two thousand years ago, God Himself offered the perfect sacrifice on our behalf—His own beloved Son. As a reflection of this ultimate sacrifice, Romans 12:1 tells us, *"I beseech you therefore, brethren, by the mercies of God, that ye present your bodies a living sacrifice, holy, acceptable unto God, which is your reasonable service."* Present our *bodies* as a free-will sacrifice? Yes, that is indeed what this passage is asking of us, as followers of the Lamb. We are told to present our bodies as a living and breathing sacrifice to Him—a free-will offering—for *"by Him were all things created"* (Colossians 1:17). Our life is the greatest thing we can offer to our Savior in spiritual worship. Pouring out ourselves to Him—*"that the life also of Jesus might be made manifest in our body"* (II Corinthians 4:10)—is the only service of worship which is satisfactory to God the Father. It is the sacrifice of our *all*, just as the woman who came to Jesus on the eve of His crucifixion worshipped Him with the most costly gift she had (Matthew 26:7)—an alabaster box of ointment. She brought to Christ tears with which she washed her Master's feet; she dried His feet not with a towel, but with the hair of her own head. She poured out that fragrance upon His precious feet as her sacrifice of worship. Are we willing to pour out *our* all before the feet of Jesus our Lord?

in *Christ alone*

On our own merit, no worship we could ever muster would be worthy of our magnificent King. We are sinful, we are creatures of His hands—how can anything we offer to the Lord be worthy of His greatness? We could not even offer our bodies as a worthy sacrifice of worship—except through His own impeccable Son, Who has redeemed us and made us worthy of such a calling (II Thessalonians 1:11). Through Christ, God now can accept our worship, not because it makes us feel good, or does Him a favor, but because the imputed righteousness of His Son rests upon us. The perfect Lamb of God is both the reason and means of our worshipful life.

Since our only hope for admissible worship is in the cleansing person of Jesus Christ, *"Who did no sin, neither was guile found in His mouth"* (I Peter 2:22), we must live in obedience to Him alone and in the shadow of His will. We must be poured out before Him, broken and surrendered. He is our Redeemer, so therefore, He is also our owner and guide (I Corinthians 6:19). We can never honor our holy God by looking to ourselves for spiritual strength; how can we, being evil, produce any acceptable thing? John 15:4 points out, *"As the branch cannot bear fruit of itself, except it abide in the vine; no more can ye, except ye abide in Me."* Romans 7:18 says, *"I know that in me (that is, in my flesh,) dwelleth no good thing,"* and Isaiah 64:6 reminds us, *"We are all as an unclean thing, and all our righteousnesses are as filthy rags; and we all do fade as a leaf; and our iniquities, like the wind, have taken us away."* We can all relate to Paul's expressions in Romans 7:19-20, *"The good that I would I do not: but the evil which I would not, that I do."* How keenly I have felt my own inability to offer any sacrifice of value to my holy God; at one point of discouragement in my spiritual walk, the Lord spoke to my heart when a friend reminded me, "Discouragement with self is just an indication that we think we can get something good out of ourselves; we cannot. Our goodness is wrapped up in the person of the Lord Jesus." Oh, that this fact would be ever present in my mind: through Christ alone can I attain any good thing. When I take my eyes from Him, and instead strive to offer something good through my own strength, I meet utter failure. What is there profitable to behold within myself? Who wants to look at a decaying corpse? Colossians 3:3 says, *"For ye are dead, and your life is hid with Christ in God,"* and Christ has promised, *"My grace is sufficient for thee: for My strength is made perfect in weakness"* (II Corinthians 12:9). Therefore, may we ever look to the One Who *lives*—Christ in us. What a Gospel is ours, that our Emmanuel[4] equips us to worship Him clothed in *His own* righteousness! Truly, He is the Author and Finisher of our faith (Hebrews 12:2). We can fully rest in the fact that Christ is able to conform us to His image, and has promised to do so in Philippians 1:6: *"Being confident of this very thing, that He which hath begun a good work in you will perform it until the day of Jesus Christ."* Oh, what glorious truth found in Romans 7:24-25: *"Who shall deliver me from the body of this death? I thank God through Jesus Christ our Lord."*

> We are never anywhere commanded to behold our emotions, nor our experiences, nor even our sins, but we are commanded to turn our backs upon all these, and to behold the *Lamb of God.*
>
> (HANNAH W. SMITH)

Though we were born with a heart full of wicked desires, Christ Jesus renews our heart in redemption. As Ezekiel 36:26

---

[4] EMMANUEL. *The God Who is with us (Matthew 1:23).*

explains, "*A new heart also will I give you, and a new spirit will I put within you: and I will take away the stony heart out of your flesh, and I will give you an heart of flesh.*" Jesus took out our old stoney heart, and replaced it with a new heart sensitive to His will. He also promised to "*put My spirit within you, and cause you to walk in My statutes, and ye shall keep my judgments, and do them*" (Ezekiel 36:27). As one friend explained to me, "We have had a heart transplant with a pace-maker added for good measure: that pace-maker is the Holy Spirit, that He puts within us to cause us to walk in His ways." Thus, our "*old man is crucified with [Christ], that the body of sin might be destroyed, that henceforth we should not serve sin*" (Romans 6:6). Our spiritual rebirth causes us to have new desires with the Holy Spirit to guide our old body of flesh—"*If any man be in Christ, he is a new creature: old things are passed away; behold, all things are become new*" (II Corinthians 5:17).

This is the reason that a regenerated, born-again Christian encounters a struggle with his own flesh. In Romans chapter seven, Paul explains that when we were unsaved, we did not struggle with the desires of our flesh, for we served them. "*When ye were the servants of sin, ye were free from righteousness*" (Romans 6:20-21). However, when we are given a new heart by Christ, we have a new purpose—to obediently walk in the ways of our holy Father—and that means we must deny our fleshly desires. "*Now being made free from sin, and become servants to God, ye have your fruit unto holiness, and the end everlasting life*" (Romans 6:22). Therefore we are "*dead indeed unto sin, but alive unto God through Jesus Christ our Lord*" (Romans 6:11). Spiritual conversion means a completely changed life, a commencement of a journey walking with Jesus. He alone offers the grace for us to walk victoriously in a body of flesh. We are alive through Christ Jesus, as His holiness is lived out in us (Romans 6:11).

Before our redemption, sin was an innate habit in our life, and though we are now free from serving those condemning passions, the work of transformation and sanctification (Romans 8:29) in our lives does not happen instantaneously or effortlessly. As Christ's crucifixion was a slow and painful death, so the annulment[5] of our fleshly, sinful desires will be gradually enervated[6] over the course of our lifetime, until we are freed from it in Heaven (Romans 6:7). *"They that are Christ's have crucified the flesh with the affections and lusts"* (Galatians 5:24). In this earthly journey, we are called to subject ourselves to the mastery of our spiritual Head (Colossians 1:18), Who offered Himself up as our sacrifice. Thus, He can renew and purify our passions and desires—retraining us in ways of His righteousness, until that bright and glorious day when *"we shall all be changed, in a moment, in the twinkling of an eye, at the last trump"* (I Corinthians 15:52), and at last *"we shall be like Him; for we shall see Him as He is"* (I John 3:2). *"I will sing of mercy and judgment: unto Thee, O LORD, will I sing"* (Psalm 101:1).

> By lamenting our weakness have we ever become more *strong?* Let us look to Jesus and His *strength* will communicate itself to our hearts, His *praise* will break forth from our lips.
>
> (THEODORE MONOD)

tower of strength

As we live out the journey of worship, we must always be seeking out our Lord's will for our lives. What a blessing is given to us through His Word, for therein we can learn how to wor-

---

[5] ANNUL. *To reduce to nothing; to obliterate.*

[6] ENERVATE. *To deprive of nerve, force, or strength.*

ship Him and live in a manner which is well-pleasing to Him. Because His *"commandment is a lamp; and the law is light"* (Proverbs 6:23), we must immerse our minds and hearts constantly in it, that we would be guided by its principles in every decision. The Bible offers answers for the choices we must face in this life. I Corinthians chapter six gives some basic principles by which to steer when standing at these crossroads:

- ∽ Is this beneficial to my spiritual, mental, and physical life? *"All things are lawful unto me, but all things are not expedient."* (verse 12)

- ∽ Does it bring me under its power? *"I will not be brought under the power of any."* (verse 12)

- ∽ Would Jesus Christ do this Himself? *"Know ye not that your bodies are the members of Christ? shall I then take the members of Christ, and make them the members of an harlot? God forbid."* (verse 15)

- ∽ Does this glorify my God and Savior? *"What? know ye not that your body is the temple of the Holy Ghost which is in you, which ye have of God, and ye are not your own?"* (verse 19)

We are not our own, but bought with the priceless blood of the Son of God (I Peter 1:19); therefore, Christ's Word must be our preeminent standard and motivation at every turn. As we keep His commands, He is pleased, for I John 2:3 says, *"Hereby we do know that we know Him, if we keep His commandments."* Obedience is our sacrifice of true, worthy worship.

path of obedience

Although as a child of God, we are freed from the bondage of sin and death (Romans 8:2), we still have a "bent posture" toward sin. To obey God's will in our spiritual sacrifice of worship, our sinful passions must be vitiated,[7] for Proverbs 14:12 soberly reminds, *"There is a way which seemeth right unto a man, but the end thereof are the ways of death."* Our hearts must be trained in *"the obedience of Christ"* (II Corinthians 10:5) to delight in His way (Psalm 37:4-7). We have the responsibility to avoid sinful propensities[8] and temptations (Ephesians 5:11). This is where the rubber meets the road, so to speak; this is when our will comes in and we must choose which path we will take. For example, if you have found that reading a certain book or an activity hinders your focus on Christ or arouses sinful passions, you must run from it. Do not allow yourself this fleshly desire, for *"the spirit indeed is willing, but the flesh is weak"* (Matthew 26:41). As Jerry Bridges says in *The Pursuit of Holiness*, "Each of us should seek to be aware of how sin attacks us through our desires, and take preventative actions." Imagine that you walk into a room and spot a cookie on the table, which is designated for a specific person. If you are not supposed to partake of it, then you would not want to hover around it, play with it, feel it, or smell it; but rather, you should move away from it. Similarly, you must *"flee also youthful lusts,"* and instead, *"follow righteousness, faith, charity, peace, with them that call on the Lord out of a pure heart"* (II Timothy 2:22). How can you knowingly walk into sin, or "play" around it, when the Holy Spirit has convicted you that it is a transgression against Jesus Christ your Lord? God forbid that we willingly sin (Romans 6:15)! Allowing yourself to go unguarded into known temptation "just once" paves a path for failure—essentially, disobedience to the Lord. We cannot expect God's blessing if we are knowingly *choosing* to walk into a path of sin, rejecting the

---

[7] VITIATE. *To render defective; to destroy.*

[8] PROPENSITY. *Bent inclination; disposition to any thing good or evil.*

strength He offers to overcome iniquity in our heart (II Corinthians 12:9). As Mary Slessor warned, "If you play with temptation, do not expect God will deliver you."

It is helpful to create a "plan of attack" for those areas in our lives with which we battle; if we know that we are weak in a certain area, then we can purpose to respond in a God-honoring way. For example, when I face a wrong desire, I can purpose to first, stop immediately; secondly, refute[9] the sinful desire by not letting my mind dwell on it; and thirdly, turn my thoughts to prayer and Scripture recitation. Making a plan for those areas of known weakness of my flesh, is very helpful for the walk of obedience to the will of the Lord. Galatians 6:8 says, *"For he that soweth to his flesh shall of the flesh reap corruption; but he that soweth to the Spirit shall of the Spirit reap life everlasting."*

The Holy Spirit is a guide to our hearts, and we must be immediately sensitive and obedient to His leading, desiring to please and obey Christ in all things. *"Grieve not the holy Spirit of God, whereby ye are sealed unto the day of redemption,"* says Ephesians 4:30. If we choose to disobey the prompting of God's will, we are inviting the consequences of our sin and God's chastisement in our life. Hebrews 12:6 says that *"whom the Lord loveth He chasteneth,"* and continues that this is for *"our profit, that we might be partakers of His holiness."* To share an example from my life, at one time I was struggling with discontent and unholy thoughts, though the Lord faithfully convicted me through I Peter 1:13 of my lack of obedience to His will: *"Wherefore gird up the loins of your mind, be sober."* In my sin, I did not want to annul this "fleshly provision"; I did not *want* to rid my mind of these momentarily gratifying, although ultimately damaging, thoughts. Because I did not obey the Holy Spirit's prompting initially, but

---

[9] REFUTE. *To disprove or overthrow.*

rather allowed the sin to grow daily stronger, consequences followed in the fruitfulness of my walk with Christ. When I finally
saw how this growing weed was damaging my spiritual life, and
turned my steps, the journey of rebuilding close communion
with the Lord was definitely a battle. Repeatedly those temptations had to be shunned—yet how merciful is my Lord, Who
promises grace in my weakness and cleansing power to wash me
whiter than snow: *"Purge me with hyssop, and I shall be clean: wash
me, and I shall be whiter than snow"* (Psalm 51:7). It is not worth
the temporal satisfaction or fleshly pleasure to continue in sin,
when Christ has offered such higher spiritual rewards for our
obedience to heed His voice. Friend, promptly heed the Holy
Spirit's conviction, for He is given as a Guide in the way of righteousness (John 16:13).

freedom of obedience

Living for the Lord of lords (I Timothy 6:15) is freeing
indeed, for we are no longer slaves to our own damning sin
and lusts (Romans 8:2). Paul explained our salvation, *"When
we were in the flesh, the motions of sins, which were by the law, did
work in our members to bring forth fruit unto death. But now we are
delivered from the law, that being dead wherein we were held; that we
should serve in newness of spirit"* (Romans 7:5-6). Although choosing to walk in obedience to Christ and His will is a daily climb,
contrary to our own natural desires, He has offered perfect
strength and deliverance for each battle: *"There hath no temptation taken you but such as is common to man: but God is faithful,
who will not suffer you to be tempted above that ye are able; but will
with the temptation also make a way to escape, that ye may be able to
bear it"* (I Corinthians 10:13). He has given us "hind's feet" to
scale these mounts of difficulty (II Samuel 22:31,33-34).

Psalm 37:4-6 offers blessing to those who choose to walk in God's way: *"Delight thyself also in the LORD; and He shall give thee the desires of thine heart...Commit thy way unto the LORD; trust also in Him; and He shall bring it to pass. And He shall bring forth thy righteousness as the light, and thy judgment as the noonday."* That final promise—that Christ shall bring forth our righteousness as the light—brings such bounteous hope for the commands in the preceding verses. As we delight in His path and commit ourselves to walking in obedience, He shall bring forth righteousness in us—which, of course, should be our ultimate desire, that He be glorified through our lives (II Corinthians 4:11).

cleaving unto our God

One morning as I was reading the book of Joshua, I encountered his command to the Israelites, *"Cleave unto the LORD your God, as ye have done unto this day"* (Joshua 23:8). This exhortation struck me and I wondered, *How do I "cleave" to the Lord?* Looking this term up in a concordance, I noticed that the first reference of "cleave"[10] occurred in Genesis 2:24, speaking of the marriage relationship, in which the man and woman are to be joined as *one* flesh. The Lord God often referred to Israel as His chosen bride, and His covenant with His people is eternal. His faithfulness to His people is never wavering, and He desired them to be "one with Him." As His children, we are the bride of Christ (Isaiah 62:5), therefore we are called to "cleave" to Him as our Lord, as part of His body. *"Ye are the body of Christ,"* says I Corinthians 12:27. We are one with Him, just as Christ is united with His Father; *"I and my Father are one"* (John 10:30).

The concept of cleaving to the Lord is more than fleshly, for

---

[10] CLEAVE. *To stick; to adhere. To unite or be united closely in interests or affection.*

it must involve our heart. Imagine if you were to tape yourself to your sister one day to see what "cleaving" looks like in the flesh. Although you might be bodily inseparable from her, you could yet resent every decision she makes. However, in Jesus Christ's example, He is one with God and He *agreed* with the Father by submitting Himself to Him. Similar should be our "cleaving" to our Savior; we willingly must go with Him and speak His Words, saying, *"I delight to do Thy will, O my God"* (Psalm 40:8).

If we delight in our Father and are closely cleaving with Him, we will love to do His will, which is to *"love the Lord thy God with all thy heart, and with all thy soul, and with all thy mind"* (Matthew 22:37-39). Our heart's unmixed adoration should be for the Lord our God (Deuteronomy 10:12, Mark 12:30), for He created and redeemed us (I Corinthians 6:20).

Our love for our Redeemer is manifested by our obedience to His commands, for II John 1:6 says, *"This is love, that we walk after His commandments."* How can we say that we love the Lord, if we do not prove that by actions which honor Him? If we say to our parents, "I love you!" and then turn around and disobey their desires, we are demonstrating to them that we actually do *not* love them (I John 4:20).

By honoring the will of God—joyfully walking in step with Him as we cleave to Him—we demonstrate our worshipful adoration, because through our obedience to His will and relinquishment of our own, we acknowledge that His way is higher than our own, that we are willing to lay our desires on the altar in faith, and that we will trust His promises to all who obey. Once again, these are the steps of an unfeigned[11] life of worship.

---

[11] UNFEIGNED. *Not counterfeit; real; sincere.*

the greatest of these

Following His command to us to love the Lord God with all of our hearts, Christ continued in Matthew 22:39, *"Thou shalt love thy neighbour as thyself."* This is the heart of our Father—and if we are "cleaving" to Him, it will also be our heart's desire, and will be lived out through our actions. In this fruitfulness of love, the Lord is exalted, for in John 15:8 He said, *"Herein is my Father glorified, that ye bear much fruit,"* and continued to that end, *"as the Father hath loved Me, so have I loved you: continue ye in My love."*

What is God's love like? How do we "continue in it"? A study of God's love is a quest worth dedicating an entire lifetime to—so widespread is its vast shores! The roots of true love are firmly grounded in the character of God, for He is its source. His ultimate demonstration of love is seen in His love for His Son; He created entire worlds as a gift for Christ (Colossians 1:19).

> *study* I Corinthians 13—how you can apply it in daily life? How do you love God more? How can you show His *love* toward others?

The eternal God further manifested His love toward mankind—a sorry lot who merited no affection, let alone atonement and reconciliation[12]—when He made us heirs with Christ, His well-loved Son (Romans 8:17). I John 3:1 revels in this glorious fact: *"Behold, what manner of love the Father hath bestowed upon us, that we should be called the sons of God."* What sacrifice God's love for us demanded—the death of His precious Son. Herein we

---

[12] RECONCILIATION. *The means by which sinners are reconciled and brought into a state of favor with God, after natural estrangement or enmity.*

see a portrayal of true love; it is nothing like the emotional, sentimental type of love depicted and promoted in our modern culture. God Almighty *chose* to love us with an unchanging and non-merited affection, which was ultimately sacrificial. There was nothing within us to earn or deserve this unspeakable gift. Through Christ, God's love will never be separated from us, for Romans 8:38-39 says, *"Neither death, nor life, nor angels, nor principalities, nor powers, nor things present, nor things to come, nor height, nor depth, nor any other creature, shall be able to separate us from the love of God, which is in Christ Jesus our Lord."* That is true love—a commitment that changes not, no matter how we fail Him. What a peace-giving truth this is!

a conduit of love

We are called to dispense the love of God to others through our lives, for as I John 4:20 points out, *"If a man say, I love God, and hateth his brother, he is a liar: for he that loveth not his brother whom he hath seen, how can he love God whom he hath not seen?"* How can we say we love God if we do not love our "brothers" as He commands?

The love of God poured out through us, once again, is not sentiment and emotion. Rather, it is the essence of Christ's inexhaustible river of love shown at the Cross. John 15:13 explains, *"Greater love hath no man than this, that a man lay down his life for his friends"*—and obviously Jesus gave us this ultimate example by laying down *His* life for His people. Just as we see throughout Christ's life in the Gospels, love pours out an unaltered, ceaseless fountain, no matter who the recipient is... no matter how difficult they may be to love...no matter if it is noticed, returned, appreciated, thought well of, or judged...no matter how it is shunned, mocked, or despised (Romans 12:14).

It keeps giving and giving. Love *never* fails, as I Corinthians 13 beautifully describes: *"Charity suffereth long, and is kind; charity envieth not; charity vaunteth not itself, is not puffed up, doth not behave itself unseemly, seeketh not her own, is not easily provoked, thinketh no evil; rejoiceth not in iniquity, but rejoiceth in the truth; beareth all things, believeth all things, hopeth all things, endureth all things. Charity never faileth."* God's love within us is aggressive!

Walking in love is a sacrificial choice; it is proven true by service, self-denial, labor, and sweat—the laying down of our lives for the sake of Christ. Serving the poor and needy, listening to a burdened soul, showing patience in the midst of suffering, demonstrating acceptance in the place of bitterness, rejoicing in truth despite adverse circumstances, pouring out ourselves to others until it hurts—these evidences of Christ's love are blessed by the Lord and exalt His worthiness. In this outpouring of love to others, we are a display of Jesus Christ to the world (I John 4:12).

> True *godliness* is not based on how many spiritual disciplines we "check off the list." Rather, it is a *manifestation* of Jesus in us when we are "bumped" by the trials of life.

Ephesians 5:2 says, *"Walk in love, as Christ also hath loved us, and hath given Himself for us an offering and a sacrifice to God for a sweetsmelling savour."* Our humble sacrifices of sincere worship do not have to be offered "on stage" for Jesus to be glorified (James 4:10), for He sees and honors our humble obedience. He takes joy in our love-demonstrations, offered in gratitude for His sacrifice on the Cross (Colossians 3:11).

In John 15:5, we are told, *"I am the vine, ye are the branches:*

He that abideth in Me, and I in him, the same bringeth forth much fruit: for without Me ye can do nothing." "Abiding" means "to remain"—we must live our lives in the arena of God's love to bear its fruit. Our lives must be hidden in the true Vine and His Word for His likeness to be poured out through us. As when a sweet fruit is crushed and spills forth a savory perfume, so is the Christian who is walking in the sweet love of the Lord going to "spill Him forth." The pressures, trials, or sufferings of life will bring forth the essence of *Christ's* spirit within us. That "aroma" is described in Galatians 5:22-23: *"The fruit of the Spirit is love, joy, peace, longsuffering, gentleness, goodness, faith, meekness, temperance: against such there is no law."* This fruit is a well-pleasing fragrance to our Lord.

anchor of joy

The Lord's blessings upon those who cleave unto Him and abide in His love are overflowing. John says, *"If ye keep My commandments, ye shall abide in My love,"* and then continues with the beautiful promise—*"these things have I spoken unto you, that My joy might remain in you, and that your joy might be full"* (John 15:10-11). Christ desires that our "joy might be full," and indeed brimming with joy is the one who is in step with His will. As we bear about the dying of the body of Christ (II Corinthians 4:10), the joy of the Lord will be our strength (Nehemiah 8:10). The results of a life of obedient, God-glorifying worship is the filling of His unspeakable joy. As His daily, constant provision sustains in our lives (Psalm 116:12) and enables our sacrifices of worship, our tongues can never cease to proclaim thanksgiving for His mercies. Psalm 35:28 proclaims, *"My tongue shall speak of Thy righteousness and of Thy praise all the day long."* The result of a life of worship?—inexpressible joy and continual proclamation of Jehovah-Jireh's outpoured goodness—for the Lord, alone, truly is our provider!

What exactly is the joy of the Lord? Is it a warm feeling or happy emotion? The book of Philippians spills forth exhortations on the theme of joy, yet by the inspiration of the Holy Spirit (II Peter 1:21) was authored by a man who faced some of the most excruciating physical trials: afflictions, ship wrecks, snake bites, stripes, imprisonings, persecutions, and more (Acts 16:23, II Corinthians 6:5). That sounds like a pretty bleak set of hardships to bear! Yet while he was bound in chains, Paul himself commanded, *"My brethren, rejoice in the Lord"* (Philippians 3:1). How could this apostle rejoice exceedingly in the midst of such painful opposition, when his future looked so desolate? The reason for his joy was because his hope, his knowledge, and his eternal future stemmed not from any earthly pleasure, but from the core being of his life—Jesus Christ.

Joy is not an emotion of happiness nor a cheap worldly thrill—but it is the anchor of hope founded deep in our souls. This hope is rested in the knowledge that we are Christ's and nothing can ever take us from His grasp (Romans 8:35). Joy is based in the One Who changes not (Malachi 3:6) and sustains us even in the darkest moments, for although *"weeping may endure for a night,"* we are promised that *"joy cometh in the morning"* (Psalm 30:5). Though we often encounter the pain obedience's sacrifice to the Lord, His joy can still always be ours, because His immutable[13] character and His commands remain unchanging. We must choose to walk in obedience Christ, no matter what oppositions or emotions we encounter. We must climb mount Moriah like Abraham did, offer to God our sacrifice of obedience, and as we lay our own will there on

---

[13] IMMUTABLE. *Unchanging; not capable or susceptible of change.*

the altar, walk in light of what He has revealed in the Word. For our obedience, the Lord grants His perfect joy.

making the choice

Psalm 56 offers an example to us for the times when faith's journey is obscured, for when David penned this passage, he was in great physical distress. He expressed his discouragement, *"Mine enemies would daily swallow me up: for they be many that fight against me, O Thou most High. What time I am afraid, I will trust in Thee."* This was a courageous man who had faced the giant Goliath audaciously and conquered many in fearsome combat, yet here when he was being chased by Saul and pursued by the Philistines, he admitted, "I am afraid." However, in spite of his fear, also note his commitment: "I *will* trust in Thee." David did not despond over his humanly hopeless situation. He chose

> You can will to...*obey* the will of God when no comfortable glow of *emotion* accompanies your obedience.
>
> (ELIZABETH PRENTISS)

to—with his will—trust in his God, continuing to recall his Shepherd's promises and faithfulness. He reminisced, *"In the LORD will I praise His word... For Thou hast delivered my soul from death: wilt not Thou deliver my feet from falling, that I may walk before God in the light of the living?"* "I will"—that is a key. "I *will* praise the Lord, for He *is* faithful."

I remember one day when I felt discouraged; though I did not "feel like" praising the Lord, I flipped to Psalm 116 and began to pray, *Father, I feel far from Your side at this moment, but I know You are there and have not moved one step, for Your promises of truth and love are the same. I will offer to Thee the sacrifice of thanksgiving, for I know that You are gracious, and righteous; yea, even greatly merciful. I love You, LORD, because You have heard my voice and have saved me from the pit. Therefore will I call upon You as long as I live.* Indeed, as I continued to obey the Lord in His commands to rejoice evermore (1 Thessalonians 5:15) and reflect on His truth (Lamentations 3:24) as diligently as when I "felt" joyful, His joy was made more real to my heart.

Though our circumstances, emotions, and feelings constantly change, our omnipresent El Shaddai—the One Who is with me wherever I go and Who is able to meet my every need—never wavers, for James 1:17 says that with Him there "*is no variableness, neither shadow of turning.*" He cannot change, or do anything like changing in the slightest way. We can rest in His immutability, and His joy will truly be our strength and our soul's steady anchor (read Psalm 100). Joy is unhindered by the storms of life, for we know that we are safe in the hands of One Who will guide us Home (John 17:24). Who can cease to sing the praises of the Eternal One's goodnesses (Hebrews 13:15)? We as Christians should most of all be a people of praise, for His provision through the Lamb (Deuteronomy 26:19). "*Thou wilt shew me the path of life: in Thy presence is fulness of joy; at Thy right hand there are pleasures for evermore*" (Psalm 16:11).

> Joy is the result of our obedience to trust, *rejoice* in, and obey the Lord in *all* circumstances.

a sacrifice well-pleasing

Our lives of sacrificial worship fill the throne room of God with a pleasing aroma of His Son: *"We are unto God a sweet savour of Christ"* (II Corinthians 2:15). Because the Lamb once slain offered His *all*—not on Mount Moriah—but on the cross of Calvary, let us offer up to Him *our* all: the sacrifice of our lives and service (I Chronicles 29:14). For this is an offering well-pleasing in His sight! *"That the trial of your faith, being much more precious than of gold that perisheth, though it be tried with fire, might be found unto praise and honour and glory at the appearing of Jesus Christ: Whom having not seen, ye love"* (I Peter 1:7-8).

"Who can refuse to adore

the Prince of perfection,

the Mirror of beauty,

the majestic Son of God?"

c h a r l e s   s p u r g e o n

"worthy is the Lamb
that was slain

to receive power, and riches, and wisdom,

and strength, and honour, and

glory & blessing."

∼

revelation 5:12

SIX

facedown

*T*HE QUEST of knowing our King and Redeemer more fully is a captivating joy which will continue throughout eternity. The glimpses of our Father and Savior found in the Scriptures offer only a foretaste of His infinite character and glory, which will be further revealed to us in Heaven. Christ Jesus has promised to us eternal life, that we may abide with Him forever; through His finished work on the cross, our sins are covered so that we can dwell in His presence. In John 17:24, Christ prayed, *"Father, I will that they also, whom thou hast given Me, be with Me where I am; that they may behold My glory."* Oh glorious day, when we will bow as we meet our Daystar seated on the right hand of God (Colossians 3:1)—the Son Who died in our stead, that we may enter into His presence faultless (Jude 1:24)! The habitation of this holy God will not be defiled by any corruption (Revelation 21:27) and nothing will distract from His holiness. His glistening glory will be unfurled as an emerald rainbow around His throne (Revelation 4:3-6) and will mesmerize our wondering eyes. On that everlasting day, our voices will never grow hoarse as we join the twenty-four elders and the hosts of angels in joyful praise to this One Who is worthy of all—*"Blessing, and honour, and glory, and power, be unto Him that sitteth upon the throne, and unto the Lamb for ever and ever"* (Revelation 5:13).

My heart leaps with joy at the thought of this soon-coming day, when my soul will be enabled to ceaselessly sing the praises of my righteous God and Savior throughout all of eternity! This hope spurs me to seek and serve Christ the Lamb with greater zeal in the short marathon of life—to *"press toward the mark for the prize of the high calling of God in Christ Jesus"* (Philippians 3:14). Though earthly battles may seem to tarry long, in light of God's promises to those who know Him (Hebrews 11:6), this life is just a vanishing blink. However, it is also a rich opportunity to store up for the glory of Heaven, for *"when the chief Shepherd shall appear,"* we *"shall receive a crown of glory that fadeth not away"* (I Peter 5:4). Every infinitesimal, minor trial encountered in this world will only add to the glory of that incorruptible prize (I Corinthians 9:25). II Corinthians 4:17 says that *"our light affliction, which is but for a moment, worketh for us a far more exceeding and eternal weight of glory."* James 1:12 promises, *"Blessed is the man that endureth temptation: for when he is tried, he shall receive the crown of life, which the Lord hath promised to them that love Him."*

On that bright day when we meet our Savior face to face, may it not be one of regrets, longing that we had served and loved our Savior more passionately. Rather, let us press forward with valor and vigor, honoring our Lord with all of our strength, in order to gain the prize of the glory of Jesus Christ, suffering what may come and enduring in faith until the end. Our unalloyed love for the Lord God will reap an eternal crown laden with glory. Our Master encourages us, *"Be thou faithful unto death, and I will give thee a crown of life"* (Revelation 2:10).

Our ultimate joy will be found in casting this crown of glory back to Jesus—the One Who laid aside His robes of glory to ransom us from hell; the One Who wore a crown of thorns on Calvary (Matthew 27:29) that He could bring us to His holy Place; the One to Whom all praise is due! *"Thou art worthy, O Lord, to receive glory and honour and power: for Thou hast created all things, and for Thy pleasure they are and were created"* (Revelation 4:11). May we lay up for that everlasting prize which shall be given unto those that love the Lord (II Timothy 4:8), so that on that great day, we may give it to the only One worthy of it—the Lamb crowned with splendor and clothed in majesty (Isaiah 33:17).

Let us seek to know this King of Glory, and follow in His footsteps until that day when we will gaze upon His precious face. In this life, may we only pursue one thing—to know Christ more. *"Now unto Him that is able to keep you from falling, and to present you faultless before the presence of His glory with exceeding joy, to the only wise God our Saviour, be glory and majesty, dominion and power, both now and ever. Amen"* (Jude 1:24-25).

"Blessing, and glory, and wisdom,
& thanksgiving, and honour, and
power, and might, be unto our
God for ever and ever. Amen."

revelation 7:12

"Bless the LORD, O my soul,

and *forget not* all His benefits:

Who forgiveth all thine iniquities;

Who healeth all thy diseases;

Who *redeemeth* thy life from destruction.

For as the heaven is high above the earth,

so great is His mercy toward them that *fear him*."

p s a l m   1 0 3

"Only one life, 'twill soon be past,

Only what's done *for Christ* will last.

And when I am dying, how happy I'll be,

If the *lamp* of my life has been

burned out for Thee."

c .   t .   s t u d d

spiritual food
FOR PERSONAL REVIVAL

- ～ Exposit God's Word daily—keep a concordance, and a dictionary handy as you study the Scriptures prayerfully.
- ～ Journal the Lord's character traits revealed in the Word.
- ～ Memorize Scripture daily, with accountability.
- ～ Develop an effective, Biblically-based prayer life.
- ～ Make the Scriptures constantly visible in your life.
- ～ Frequently listen to Christ-exalting sermons while you work, exercise, or perform routine duties.
- ～ Ask your mother or another godly "Titus 2" woman to keep you spiritually accountable and to pray for you.
- ～ Read about godly men and women who served Christ with their all (for example, Jonathan & Sarah Edwards, David Brainerd, William Wilberforce, George Mueller, R. A. Torrey, Hudson Taylor, Adoniram & Ann Judson, John & Betty Stam, Frances Havergal, Jim & Elisabeth Elliot, Amy Carmichael, Isobel Kuhn, Lilias Trotter, and countless others). Many books written by or about missionaries are out of print, but are freely available online.
- ～ Pray daily and continue hourly, seeking to commune constantly with Christ Jesus (Colossians 3:16).

"Open thy mouth wide, and *I will fill it.*"

psalm 81:10

appendix II

personal evaluations
BASED ON CHRIST'S
TEACHINGS IN MATTHEW

⌒Am I willing to be governed by Christ in all things? Is a quality of brokenness visible in my daily life? (5:3)

⌒Am I mourning over sin in my life with a sorrow that leads to godly repentance? (5:4)

⌒Do I place Christ daily first in my life, meekly laying my will on the altar in any given situation? (5:5)

⌒Do I hunger after righteousness in my life (Psalm 104:34)? (5:6) If not, then how much time am I spending with Christ every day? Am I putting the Word first in my life, making sure nothing is hindering my focus for Jesus? Does my thirst for Him create a hunger for God in the lives of others? (5:13)

⌒Do I show a spirit of mercy toward others, as Christ has shown toward me? (5:7)

⌒Have I laid down all other affections that I have cherished more than Christ? Do I have a single-minded devotion to my Savior? (5:8)

⌒Do I truly have an attitude of love and desire to keep unity within the body of Christ? (5:9)

⌒Am I standing so strongly for the Lord that I face fierce opposition from the world? (5:10-12)

⌒Is every aspect of my life a bright reflection of Jesus in opposition to a dark world? (5:13)

⁓Is there anyone who has something against me whom I have not approached in reconciliation? (5:23)

⁓Do I bless those who oppose and persecute me? (5:44)

⁓When I pray, do I desire to be seen or to impress others? (6:5)

⁓Am I constantly refraining from worldly issues that obscure my spiritual focus on Jesus Christ? Am I willing to give up anything for Him at a moment's notice? (6:16)

⁓Where do my thoughts reside, as a result of the books and other media I have exposed myself to? (6:21)

⁓Am I seeking the Lord consistently, looking to Him for fulfillment? (7:7-11)

⁓Are the words I write conduits of what God is teaching me and an overflow of His Spirit, or self-centered? Does my life mirror my "Christian talk"? Do I speak of my Savior every chance I encounter? (7:5,17)

⁓Does my life "smell" like Christ—reflect the fruits of the Spirit (Galatians 5:22, Ephesians 5:9)? (7:20)

⁓Am I consistently hearing the Word of God upheld and admonished in my life? Am I closely paying attention to the godly teachings of elders in my life? (7:24)

⁓Is my life being built upon God's Word through immediate, aggressive obedience? (7:24-27)

Prayerfully evaluate your life in light of the Scriptures.

"Ye shall seek Me, and find Me,
when ye shall search for Me with *all your heart.*"

jeremiah 29:13

"The *grace*
of the Lord Jesus Christ,
and the *love* of God,
& the communion of the Holy Ghost,
be with you all. A M E N ."

II corinthians 13:14